"*Losing God* is more than a book; it is an invitation to journey into an ever-deepening experience of life's greatest passion: the passion of believing (the ever-developing decisions of faith). Faith alone opens us up to the freedoms and resulting responsibilities of loving and being loved humanly and more than humanly.

"Michael Gallagher brilliantly shows us that the journey of faith—(believing) in oneself, other(s), and the triune God—are inseparable, interdependent, and incomparable meetings of God, oneself, and one another. All else is "losing God."

"Our North American society is increasingly described as addictive and addicting because of growing individualism, better called narcissism, which has been described as the "hellishness of self-doubt." Insightfully, Gallagher describes addictiveness as a profound isolation conquered through the discovery of community, those healing spaces where the human finds solidarity, friendship, and the 'more than human.'

"Those persons seeking the Lord's invitaton to live life to the full need to consider the reading of *Losing God* as an obligation."

Msgr. Andrew Cusack, Ph.D.
Director, National Institute for Clergy Formation

"*Losing God* is really about finding God, even when we feel lost: lost in wonder, in fear, in the long journey of solitude, in conversation and community, in commitment to justice. Michael Paul Gallagher, as articulate and sensitive a man you might ever find, touches our lives with a living faith in the presence of God, found often where we least expect: at the heart of our experience. This is a lovely book."

John Kavanaugh, S.J.
Saint Louis University

LOSING

GOD

MICHAEL PAUL GALLAGHER

XXIII

TWENTY-THIRD PUBLICATIONS

Mystic, Connecticut 06355

North American Edition 1992

Originally published in 1991 as *Where Is Your God?* by Darton,
Longman and Todd Ltd., 89 Lillie Road, London.

Twenty-Third Publications
185 Willow Street
P.O. Box 180
Mystic, CT 06355
(203) 536-2611
800-321-0411

ISBN 0-89622-504-6
Library of Congress Catalog Card No. 91-67183

CONTENTS

LOSING

GOD

INTRODUCTION

Memories of Encounter

During some twenty years teaching literature at an Irish state university, I enjoyed plenty of dialogue with students, believers and non-believers alike. This book is written in the hope of continuing that conversation, in print. All those contacts with students—as both lecturer and priest—have given me whatever insights I have into the changing world of beliefs today. It has been a long, crossroads experience.

Because I grew up in a small village in western Ireland in the 1940s and 1950s, before the arrival of so-called modernity, my roots are traditional and rural. Thrown, as I was, into the totally different world of university life, I have been pushed to ponder what has been happening to people in today's culture. The students I have met were born into a different world from mine. If I had been born twenty or thirty years later I would have had to cope with much more rootlessness and more complex pressures. A steadiness for commitment would have been much harder to reach.

This book is born from my memories of those years. I want to write about some roads to faith today and I would like to do justice to the tone of that journey as I have heard it in young people I have known. It is not a simple search. It is unique for each person. It will also differ according to each situation. The notes in the faith chord struck in Latin America will sound different harmonies to those typical of Europe or North America. In recent years the biggest influence on my own faith has come from two visits to Latin America (a total of only nine months but they had a major and liberating impact on me). I want to draw on that experience and on the contrasts of faith languages I have discovered.

But the principal source for these pages lies in the hours and hours of talking with individuals I have been blessed to know over the years. Many of the sections here start from what might coldly be called "case histories." For me they are real memories of real people. Sometimes I change their names and sometimes merge stories of different people into one. But I record them all with reverence, and in the hope that they may kindle imagination and courage in others, too.

Looking back now at those hundreds of conversations over three decades, I am struck with how privileged I have been and how often those encounters helped to keep my own faith alive. I feel a huge gratitude for the trust of many young people, as they explored various areas of their human experience. Sometimes, but rarely enough, our starting point was religious. More typically we began from something of human struggles—in relationships, in families, in studies, in moods, in the decisions facing them. Frequently there was some trigger of pain that opened the door to searching and to the risk of trusting a comparative stranger. For them it was often a rare experience to be able to speak honestly or to be heard with some understanding, or just to listen to one's own unvisited depths. Gradually I came to accept that I had a gift for such encounters. I seemed to have, most of the time at least, some ability to enter into the experience of people younger than myself and to offer them some space of freedom.

As I say, most of our starting points were non-religious, but often some religious hunger found expression later on. I began to realize that this was the natural order of things: we need to be free in our humanity before we can venture into the more mysterious world of our spiritual selves. Being burdened by some hurt can block me from hope. If I am carrying some guilt, it can dent my self-worth and shut me in on myself. I need to reach some clearing in the forest in order to see things more clearly. That is the gift we can be to one another: we can offer an oasis for hearing and healing. And in my experience some such entry into self-freedom is needed before a journey toward explicit faith can be fruitful. That pattern of liberation was a main concern of my book, *Free to Believe: Ten Steps to Faith.*

Emerging from Confusion
Although I previously tried to explore the *credibility* of Christianity, now I am much more interested in its *livability*. I am thinking

less of the unbeliever than the searching believer or half-believer, less of a journey toward faith from outside than a journey from confused to more convinced faith. I am thinking of so many people who were born into some church, but who fall into a limbo of vagueness, believing that they have somehow lost God along the way. And yet they remain open to the vision they once glimpsed of Christianity. With them in mind, this book will try to locate the adventure of faith within human experience, where they may find God. So it will be less interested in the contents of the creed than in the journey toward making basic sense of God for today.

For such travelers I propose the Magi story as a marvelously rich map. In this gospel tale, so often viewed only as a Christmas story for children, I find a drama of the discovery of faith. So, the structure of this book is inspired by the Magi story. It seeks also to draw upon my own experience of different contexts for faith in today's world, especially the contrasting horizons of Latin America and the so-called Western world.

The book's title, *Losing God,* is directly related to one of the most lyrical passages in the Bible, Psalm 42. There the poet is suffering from being far from home and from the mockery of hostile people:

I have no food but tears
day and night,
as all day long I am taunted,
"Where is your God?"

His poem recalls past moments of joyful celebration surrounded by a community of believers. But the past is past. Here and now, assaulted by the voices of unbelievers, he feels vulnerable, alone, and longs to see again "the face of God—like "a deer yearns for running streams." His prayer-poem swings between desolation and hope. At times he senses a kind of "death in my bones," as if helpless before the sarcasm of the doubters. He feels, in other words, as if he has lost God. But gradually he emerges into confidence that he will be guided to the "holy mountain" and be able once more to find his language of faith.

Why so downcast,
why all these signs?
Hope in God! I will praise God still,
my Savior, my God.

The plight of that ancient poet is paralleled in so many ways today. We live in a time where the basics have shifted and where faith has gone into a kind of exile. People may have memories of moments and places where faith seemed alive, when they too, in their own way, went "to the house of God amid cries of joy." But for many who feel abandoned by God, the present can seem numb and blank. How can we emerge into hope like the psalmist? Only by confronting the question, Where is your God? with the same honesty. If we can listen to it in the tones of today, then we might move toward new trust for tomorrow. In this book I try to tell how I have witnessed the struggle of the Psalmist and the hope of the Magi in the lives of people I have known.

After Jesus had been born at Bethlehem in Judaea during the reign of King Herod, suddenly some wise men came to Jerusalem from the east asking, "Where is the infant king of the Jews? We saw his star as it rose and have come to do him homage." When King Herod heard this he was perturbed, and so was the whole of Jerusalem. He called together all the chief priests and the scribes of the people, and inquired of them where the Christ was to be born. They told him, "At Bethlehem in Judaea, for this is what the prophet wrote:

And you, Bethlehem, in the land of Judah,
you are by no means the least among the leaders of
Judah,
for from you will come a leader
who will shepherd my people Israel."

Then Herod summoned the wise men to see him privately. He asked them the exact date on which the star had appeared and sent them on to Bethlehem with the words, "Go and find out all about the child, and when you have found him, let me know, so that I too may go and do him homage." Having listened to what the king had to say, they set out. And suddenly the star they had seen rising went forward and halted over the place where the child was. The sight of the star filled them with delight, and going into the house they saw the child with his mother Mary, and falling to their knees they did him homage. Then, opening their treasures, they offered him gifts of gold and frankincense and myrrh. But they were given a warning in a dream not to go back to Herod, and returned to their own country by a different way.

Matthew 2:1-12 (NJB)

CHAPTER ONE

THE MAGI REVISITED

Waiting to place the "wise men" in the crib remains one of my vivid memories of Christmas as a child. They seemed so much more exotic than shepherds. My preference for them, I later discovered, echoed a long history of Christian imagination. The earliest representations of Christmas in the catacombs were of the Magi. The shepherds came later and never attained the same popularity with artists, at least not until the carols of the Reformation. Our ancestors in the early centuries meditated at length on that journey of the Magi and wove layers of legend around the simple story as told in Matthew's Gospel.

At first they were portrayed as astrologers with pointed Phrygian caps. The sixth-century mosaics of Ravenna named them, for the first time in the West, as Balthasar, Melchior, and Gaspar. About this same time they rose to the dignity of being kings, probably because of the mention of Psalm 72 of kings of Arabia bearing gifts. My favorite example is in the stonework of Autun Cathedral where the three are in the same bed under a large blanket, and all are wearing their crowns! An angel is waking them to point out the star. One of them is shown with eyes wide open in wonder, another half-awake, but the third remains sound asleep, as if to represent three stages of spiritual alertness in the medieval tradition.

In all the early period they were portrayed as identical figures. It is only from the twelfth century onward that the magi-kings assume individual characteristics, being depicted as the three ages of life, or as representing different races and continents of the world. From this epoch comes a delightful legend that the three met for Christmas Mass in Armenia in 54 A.D. and that they died happily within a few days, all of them being well over a hundred years old. At some point their supposed bodies turned up in Milan, but after the sack of that city in 1164, Cologne Cathedral managed to acquire the relics and they remain there still in a magnificent enameled shrine. In the late Middle Ages a Cologne breviary announced that the kings had in fact been consecrated as bishops by St. Thomas in India, thereby creating another problem for artists concerning what headgear to give them.

Apart from the legends and the art, spiritual writers reflected on the Magi in many ways. The Venerable Bede was one of those who suggested meanings for the three gifts: gold signified kingship; incense, divinity; and myrrh, a prophecy of the passion. A few centuries later St. Bernard's interpretation was more down to earth: money for the poor family; incense to disinfect the stable; and myrrh as a herbal remedy against worms in children.

In our own century the tradition continues. Two Nobel prize winning poets offered rather contrasting angles on conflict at the heart of the story. T.S. Eliot evoked a difficult journey toward a moment of costly inner conversion: this birth seemed like death for them, and so disturbed them that they were "no longer at ease" in their old vision of things. But for the Guatemalan, Miguel Angel Asturias, the white king offers gold in order that Jesus may confront the lure of wealth and power: "Even from the cradle You may see the Enemy...with You is born the grave of Gold." More recently, Ermanno Olmi, the Italian film director, has developed the Magi story at some length in *Cammina Cammina*, and I shall draw upon his work as an epilogue to this book.

Latin American Insights
With that long and fascinating history, one need not feel shy in offering yet another version of the Magi story. I had been pondering it for some years when it came into focus in a powerful way for me when I was in Venezuela. I outlined the story as a theme for reflection and prayer during some retreats for young people. They took up my suggestion and together we began to see this gospel passage as offering a rich agenda for Christian commitment. From their pooling of insights, born of prayer and of listening to one another, these are some of the angles and lights we hit upon, which served as inspiration for the chapters that follow.

The Magi's journey began with a star. To my Venezuelan friends, this was a perfect image of anything that calls people to set out on a journey toward faith. Each of us is here to seek and to be faithful to the light we see. In the drama of Latin America, that light is experienced in the cry of the oppressed, in the scandals of history that call for justice. It is also known in quieter and more personal ways, whenever a person realizes that he or she is on earth for a purpose.

It struck those young people as significant that the Magi had not traveled alone. It symbolized for them a vital element in their own faith, which was so strongly nourished in small weekly gatherings. So following the light and searching for Christ are meant to be a community journey, not a lonely quest.

What about Herod? we asked. Who is he now? *El podoroso,* was one of the replies in the group. The powerful one. The one who controls things and tries to deceive. More dangerous than an outright enemy is the dictator who pretends to be religious but who really wants to kill Christ. In Latin America, people are acutely aware of how the church can be manipulated by governments to stifle the urgency of the gospel. The conclusion of our groups was that some confrontation with Herodian systems is part of being a Christian now.

Eventually the Magi entered the house and saw the child with his mother Mary. We spoke about the places where we find Christ, and about the special role of Mary in Latin American spirituality. We paused on the idea of the house as a symbol of church. Where is the real church experienced today? Many answers flooded in: in silence, in suffering, in sacraments, in learning from the poor, in solidarity of vision, in all the struggles of the Kingdom.

One purpose of the journey of the Magi was to offer their gifts. In our reflections this became yet another symbol of the goal of faith: everyone has her or his own gift to bring to the world, for the sake of others.

For all their learning, the wise men were unaware of Herod's duplicity until they had a dream. What could that dream be for us, we asked. It would mean getting in touch with the deepest part of ourselves where the Spirit speaks. It would entail a long discernment of our world, and then a Christian dream for today could be born.

The Magi returned home by "another way." In this simple phrase we discovered a final summary of the Christian life. To have found Christ, or to have been found by Christ, leads to measuring things differently. The Kingdom is an alternative vision of what human life is about. It is utterly different from Herod's way of power and ego and death. Instead, it is a life-giving way of serving others, and of letting go of self.

There was depth in the inventiveness of the old legends that grew up around the Magi story. There is equal depth in the intuitions of those Venezuelan communities. We shall expand on those hints and re-read that gospel story as evoking an adult adventure of faith.

CHAPTER TWO

THE STAR: AWAKENING TO WONDER

What got the Magi going? St. Matthew is not forthcoming about that. All that the gospel text tells us is that these astrologers of an Eastern country saw a star in the sky and for some reason set out on a search for the newborn king. But something unusual must have struck those sky-gazers to spur them into such a risky journey. Something must have awakened their wonder and their hope.

The Bible scholars have much to tell us about the Eastern world and its assumptions, about how there were many learned experts in astrology or astronomy, about how the appearance of a marvelous star in the sky was thought to herald the birth of some great person, and so on. They also suggest that this may be a particular kind of Scripture story—*midrash*—where images of faith are more important than historical accuracy.

The puzzle still remains. Why follow the light? Why set out at all on such a quest? Perhaps answers from our own experience are as valid as any that come from expert research. To seek out the light is a basic image for any religious quest. It is a simple way of capturing what we are here for: to be faithful to conscience and experience, to follow the light we see.

But what opens our eyes to such light? How does the journey get underway?

Trusting One's Own Light

I remember how the journey started for Paul. One day he came to discuss difficulties over an essay and stayed to talk about home and parents, about feeling ungrateful, about not being able to make himself understood. Perhaps pain was the awakener: it gave him the push to explore his experience, to trust someone else with his situation.

I well remember my first conversation with Paul. What I recall most clearly is the relief he felt at being able to voice that flood of confusion inside him. Not that the home situation was one of conflict. Indeed there was great kindness from everyone there, but he felt burdened by the silence he had adopted. He also felt guilty about not responding differently. There was a kind of sadness in him because a gap had opened between him and his parents, a gap of noncommunication. So much had happened within him these last years, since coming to the university and beginning to think for himself, that it seemed as if his parents could never grasp his new language. Perhaps the trouble was that Paul had never before spoken the language of Paul to anyone. That was the breakthrough of our conversation—and a blessing for both of us. As I listened I could hear so much goodness, but goodness smothered under his own self-shadows and doubts.

At one stage I remember saying to him, "Break the magnifying glass—throw it away." I told him my theory (to be taken with a grain of salt) that the devil has a factory somewhere that specializes in manufacturing one thing only, something he delights in giving out free: a negative magnifying glass! We took a page of a book and I asked him to imagine what a magnifying glass does if one holds it over the middle of the page. It enlarges some lines or words but it distorts the rest. It was an image of Paul's experience. Like many others (including myself), he had developed a distorted picture of some of the disappointments of his life. They stood out so much that they prevented him from seeing the whole page, the whole story of his humanity. But the whole page came into view as Paul grasped the courage to express his negatives for the

first time. Paradoxically, negatives made way for positives. The
honesty over hurts opened doors to new hope, to seeing himself
with some tenderness again. Those hurts, bottled up in self-
silence, had come to loom too large for him, so talking it out gently allowed him to trust another side of himself containing the
hungers and the goodness hidden underneath the numbness.

Two Kinds of Faith

That first day's conversation was a good day's work for both of
us. It was a crucial move into freedom. I have been blessed to see
many others take a similar step out of fog into clearing of self-
clouds. What I am convinced of is that this awakening to the light
of one's own goodness often leads—as if naturally—to a more explicitly spiritual journey of faith. Perhaps faith (with a small f)
comes before Faith (with a capital F). That first "faith" is in one's
own self as worthwhile in spite of trouble—and it is this self-
worth that life often bruises. Looking back now at my years of listening, I see that I spent a lot of time fostering "faith" and trusting
that "Faith" might come into focus later on. I came to believe that
the road to "Faith" usually passes through "faith." Indeed it did
for Paul. He had to believe again in his own eclipsed goodness before he could begin the stranger adventure of believing again in
God. In "faith" he experienced the human basis of "Faith." That
was his awakening to light.

Our more explicit entry into faith language came from my
mentioning an image from the gospel, the parable of the hidden
treasure. It was as if we both stumbled across something buried in
the field. Imagine someone unearthing a box under the surface of
the soil. At first it can look dirty and one might fear that it contains just rubbish or even a dead animal. Then comes the surprise
of opening it and finding something precious. We experienced
that discovery in our listening together, and we also knew something of the second half of the parable. In Jesus' story, the person
hides the treasure again, in order to sell everything to be able to
buy the field. Even though Paul began to mention God that first

day, we were slow to enter that realm. It was as if we were both shy before this treasure we found. As someone else in similar circumstances said to me, "Faith is too important to rush into until it's ripe." I could not agree more. I have learned reverence for the rhythms of people's growth. The person in the parable went away happy, knowing the riches within the field and happy with having to wait until he or she would own it one day. We, too, ended that first exploration with a sense of gratitude for what had been already found and of more, much more, to come.

Perhaps people often awaken to the light when they have the courage to speak their pain, and to realize that there is so much more than the pain. When there is real listening, the magnifying glass can so easily be broken. Paul saw no star in the sky. He rode no camels across the desert. But our conversation echoed the excitement and intuition that got these Magi going. It was an awakening into light, and a hunch that as "faith" was being born anew in his humanity, Paul was also entering a larger and Magi-like adventure of "Faith."

The Orphanage and the Lake

Some years ago a student friend of mine surprised me one day with a story he had written. Over the previous months we had spoken a few times about faith. Andrew was going through a fair bit of questioning about religion and about his attitude to church in particular. Looking back now, perhaps much of our talking was groping in a world of *ideas*, whereas what Andrew needed was the freedom of *images*. Happily he hit upon this level of communication and came up with a parable of his own. I offer a summary of what I remember of it.

It concerned a little ten-year-old boy growing up in an orphanage. One night in the large dormitory he wakes up in the dark but knows that the dawn can't be far away. It is summer time and there is a lake on the grounds of the orphanage. He feels a great urge to see the dawn at the lakeside but the rules are rigid. On no account should any child get up before the bell and it is strictly forbidden to leave the dormitory until the proper time. But he decides to risk it. He dresses quickly and creeps out, holding his shoes in his hand so as not to awaken the others. Then there is a long corridor and—a nice touch—along it are the pictures of the past presidents of the institution on one side and of saints on the other side. So the boy puts his head down and runs down the long corridor. He does not want to be caught by the disapproving glances of the figures on the walls. He comes to the lake and waits in darkness for the dawn. The drama of day begins and the colors change from orange to red to bright sun. He watches all this reflected in the water of the lake; he is absorbed by the sheer beauty of it. Then suddenly he remembers the time. They will be up by now. He will be missed. He will be in trouble. So he gets up to return and speaks his last words to the lake, "I'll go back now. Thank you. I don't care if I'm punished because I know something now. I know that the God of the lake is greater than the God of the orphanage."

Over the years I have come back to that story as a simple but powerful evocation of where many people are concerning religion. Alas, they may have encountered only the orphanage with its rules and codes and organization. The God of the orphanage is worshipped in a religion of ritual. But the God of the lake is encountered in a way that goes beyond that into something of wonder and awe and freedom. More and more I am convinced that this is the most neglected door into faith today. There has been so much renewal, but has it really touched people on any level of depth experience?

A central struggle for us all is to reach the hunger and wonder at the core of each person, or as they say in the East, to get to the cave of the heart where the Spirit dwells. Or as Paul Tillich used to say, God is the name we give to an "inexhaustible depth" within us and any entry point to that depth is a potential road to God. It is as if each of us is a skyscraper with many floors. But we leave many of them unvisited. We fall into the habit of taking the elevator to a few limited layers of work, recreation, religious practices, all in somewhat routine fashion. Then wonder shrivels up, and we miss the moments that might awaken us for a Magi-like quest. Even the word "God" can become a distant and conventional term, one that conjures up a potentate of the universe rather than a passionate and intimate lover. The real victim of these routines is our sense of mystery. The most critical religious need today is for this experience of mystery, whatever form it might take. Let us get away from rituals and into imagination, into a poetry that can reach people's shy hunger. I call it shy because the orphanage has so often ousted the lake. It is as if the little boy was doing something shameful in seeking out the space his heart and imagination needed.

Trusting Our Depths

The spiritual intuition captured in that story can find support among theologians of today. One of my favorites is the Benedictine Sebastian Moore, who has insisted that the ineffectiveness of much organized religion is due to its failure to reach our prereligious God awareness. By this he means that the lake experience can be smothered by an over-anxious, orderly orphanage. He would hold that God lives in each person prior to our words, beliefs, or sacraments. Thus our religiousness of the spirit is deeper than our religion of the church, yet ultimately they need each other for a full language of faith.

Karl Rahner also devoted much energy to the crucial experience of mystery. Even the word "mystery" can be kidnapped and made to mean "something that cannot be understood." In its more genuinely religious meaning, it stands for something that is too rich for mere understanding. For Rahner the essential mystery is preached to us from within by God. Therefore the starting point for any faith journey has to be a person's self-experience at its deepest. It is there that everyone has a basic experience of God, if only he or she can recognize it. This is the foundation of religion through the ages, but in today's secular climate this encounter between wonder and mystery is often suppressed. There results a

kind of spiritual malnutrition, or another version of the orphanage forgetting the language of the lake. This is a danger not only
in the busy priorities of church life but, on a more academic level,
in the neglect of religious experience as a foundation for theology.

How can the lake experience be nourished? Where can we
reach this wavelength of wonder? There are many ways to awak-
en to the mystery within. Prayer is one, especially a prayer that
trusts the silence. Suffering is another when it humbles and opens
the heart. Joy is another as when a child is born or when fullness
is glimpsed through art or music. Feelings are often our best
guides. Within the last few days, I have noticed tears in the eyes
of men—a bridegroom speaking at his wedding, his brother
listening to that speech, and an illiterate drug addict, surprised
when a friend praised his sharp mind and real goodness. These
are all moments of glimpsing the depths of life. But the depths are
there whether we touch them or not.

Perhaps the examples mentioned are a little special. If so, echo-
ing St. Paul, I would suggest an even better way: wherever love is
struggled for and lived, there is the source of mystery in each life.
Love is our lake in the flow of ordinary existence. What lies behind the faces of the people you pass on the street? They may
seem tired, preoccupied, grumpy. But there is so much more. I remember a famous image in George Eliot's *Middlemarch* where she
asks a similar question: "If we had a keen vision and feeling of all
ordinary human life, it would be like hearing the grass grow and
the squirrel's heartbeat, and we should die of that roar which lies
on the other side of silence." I admire the eloquence, but my own
intuition is more positive. There are angels at work in each heart.
Too poetic? Perhaps. And yet it is my experience that on the other
side of silence, in the depths of people, there is always courage
and compassion, love and longing, even if unsure and inarticulate. Dawn at the lakeside is not only a moment of beauty in the
outer world; it has its many mirrors in the cave of each heart.

In these and many other ways the "star" continues to beckon
people. Invitations to wonder awaken us. New vistas open. Risk

now seems worthwhile. Thus faith is born when the ordinary is broken into by the extraordinary. A journey becomes possible into the known unknown. Some of the contours of such a journey will be our focus in the remainder of this book.

CHAPTER THREE

COPING WITH THE DARK

Reading between the lines of the Magi story, it seems that their experience was not one of steady light. That star did not appear and then stay shining brightly all along their journey. If that were so, they would not have had to approach Herod and his experts in Jerusalem. Nor would the sight of the star fill them with joy when they saw it again between Jerusalem and Bethlehem.

In brief, their experience was what Ruth Burrows has called the "light-on, light-off" pattern, typical of any faith journey. Everyone runs into painful patches in one way or another. So how can we cope with unsteadiness of light, with the dark times?

Can we walk wisely without the light or when it seems to have disappeared? Can we insure that darkness does not blind us to the goal of our journey?

Varieties of Burdens

I like the saying of G.K. Chesterton that faith is the art of surviving one's moods. It rings true in my experience of myself and of others. There are times when for all sorts of reasons I have practically no sense of God, no taste for prayer, and indeed little desire to do anything about it. I say "little desire" deliberately, because I think that there has always been a glimmer of hope there, some kind of trust that I will emerge from this cul-de-sac of low spirits.

Other people I have known have had to carry much heavier burdens of desolation than I have ever experienced: family tragedy, broken relationships, painful levels of anxiety or depression, or simply a blank wall of silence when they try to reach out to God. Why keep going when things seem so pointless? I have often heard some version of that cry and I have no easy answers. Faced with such genuine pain, I am always afraid of being glib, of trivializing what people experience.

But it is good to talk about the various darknesses encountered by people in their humanity and on the way of faith. These experiences are real. They can frighten and damage a person, or they can purify and give wisdom. Here I want to explore three different experiences of the dark: *the everyday darkness of the tired self; the theological darkness at the core of faith; and darkness of the doubting Thomas in ordinary life.*

The Tired Self

An image from John Powell is a useful parable of what I am calling the tired self, the temptation to judge impulsively in the dark. It tells of a man approaching his house one dark night and seeing a large snake on the front lawn. He happens to have a hatchet in his car and attacks the snake with it. It writhes and jumps around but eventually is left in bits on the ground. When the man wakes up next morning and looks out, what does he see in pieces all over the lawn but the garden hose!

Adapting that story to our purposes, the moral would seem to be: if you see snakes in the night, don't fight them. In the morning, they might turn out to be only the garden hose. We judge badly in the dark and should wait until day. It will come, even after the longest and darkest night. Whenever fatigue of spirit is in the driver's seat, it is likely to distort what you see. So beware of moods when you feel down, and wait for the return of light.

It has been a revelation for me to wait with people through the deep dark, through times when dawn seemed to have forgotten to come. Yet eventually it did come. Self-patience was important, not to mention the common sense not to kill imaginary snakes. How often just talking about desolation can raise a person's hopes! And when they have traveled their Magi path in their own way and found a sense of God in Christ, they can look back at the darker roads and see them differently. It is as if that ancient psalm (116:10-11) had come true:

> My trust does not fail even when I say,
> "I am completely wretched."
> In my terror I said,
> "No human being can be relied on."

There is a marvelous contradiction there: on one level I trust, while on another I don't. What a person says or experiences consciously does not necessarily coincide with their stronger self, the self that can survive through the dark.

Darkness of Faith

There are darknesses that come from the sufferings of life (and here, as I said, some people seem to carry heavier loads than others), but there is also an unavoidable darkness right at the heart of faith. Here is a true story about this second darkness.

At the end of a seminar on faith for teachers, a woman in her fifties expressed her gratitude for the session, which in fact had gone well. There had been a sense of real contact between me and the group. She told me that she had been a teacher of religion for some thirty years but that her own faith had been in a kind of limbo for a long time. She had always taught small children about God as if she had no doubts but, as she put it, the best she could do was to trust the great thinkers who had worked it all out, such as Thomas Aquinas or John Henry Newman. Then she drew closer to me, gripped my arm, and asked, "Are you *sure* there is a life after death?"

It was a bit terrifying to be put, even temporarily, into the same category as Aquinas or Newman. My first answer was to reach for yet another authority. I reminded her of St. Paul's strong statements that if the dead are not raised, then Christ was not raised and faith is empty, or again that if our hopes as Christians are limited to this life alone, we deserve to be looked on as fools (1 Corinthians 15:15-19). But this text was familiar to her and, understandably, was not the answer she wanted. "But are *you* sure?" she persisted. What could I say? If I said yes, it would be untrue. If I said no, it would be untrue in another way. Yes could mean a provable God, a verifiable faith, both of which seem to be to be contradictions. I had no direct data on God or on the afterlife, and the only data I have on the resurrection of Jesus derive from witnesses I have never met and from texts that cannot be checked historically in the usual way.

So I am not *sure* in the normal way of being sure. As Newman once said, "Religious light is intellectual darkness." Or to return to images of the Magi story, the light of the star that beckoned them was not comprehensible in terms of the logic of their science. It spoke to them not irrationally, but beyond their unusual reasonings. This is a way of saying why I could not unhesitatingly and honestly answer yes. My intellect in its usual way of knowing is not sure of God. God is not provable in the everyday sense of proof.

Why not, then, utter a blunt no? Because that too would be misleading. It might suggest that I am living with perpetual doubt rather than with faith. And faith is a strange kind of knowing. It is always a mixture of fragility and firmness, of incompleteness and fulfillment. It involves unsureness and sureness at one and the same time. Its sureness is not of the usual objective kind. When

the first Sputnik was sent into space, Khruschev boasted that the
astronauts found no god in the heavens. But there is another kind
of certainty, more akin to the unshakeable trust than can exist between friends than to the "proofs" that take place in laboratories
or through looking around the heavens.

The Normality of Doubts

People often surprise me with their surprise that I, a priest,
should experience unsureness about faith. They seem to think that
ordination gives some grace of steady certitude, of armor-plating
against difficulties. Alas, no. For me, brushes with darkness are
normal; at times they are deeply confusing and painful. I see no
point in hiding this. Often I find myself feeling that the whole
faith thing is utterly unreal. In certain moods I find myself buffeted by doubts about everything connected with God or Christ or
church or religion. God seems an impossibility, a tempting illusion cooked up over the centuries, born out of human needs and
surrounded by a great deal of impressive wisdom and admirable
generosity of spirit. Jesus surely existed but this extraordinary individual was later interpreted by religiously excited people in
strange ways: a myth built up around a visionary healer. The
church often appears to be a prison of dishonesty, and the real
miracle is that so much mediocrity does not alienate more people
from it. The whole history of religion seems linked with blind fa-
naticism, violence, rigid attitudes and hostility to those who break
new ground or live creatively.

Yes, I can suffer from dark thoughts and negative judgments. So
why not throw in the sponge? Why remain rooted in faith and in
the church? Negatively, because those postures always arise when I
find myself *standing outside* the life of faith, staying at a distance,
literally alienated. That is when doubting Thomas is so fascinating
as a patron saint. It is quite relevant that he was absent when the
risen Lord showed himself on Easter. Whenever I miss some worthwhile experience, and especially if it is my own fault, I am inclined
to cover my disappointment by dismissing the significance of what
others have found, even if it is only a good film or a celebration of

some kind. When Thomas missed the Lord's appearance to the others, he seems to have raised his conditions: "Unless I put my hands into his side...." At the root of such doubting is a sulking child within. Thomas had been left outside. Not until he could return to the inside, to a sense of relationship with Jesus, would he stop his negatives and voice his cry of returning faith: "My Lord and my God." Everyone has Thomas-style moments of doubt, and like him they can stem from a mixture of reactions: being annoyed with oneself, finding the witnesses incredible, and then making exaggerated demands of objectivity. So I have learned not to trust the sulking self.

More positively, I have come to recognize that reverence is a key to faith. I may have to wait through dark moods before being able to re-enter that reverence. I may have to put up with myself as I stand sulking outside. But eventually I get in touch again and rediscover a wisdom that is in tune with my deepest human experience. I have stopped being surprised by my bouts of doubt. They come and go like the weather; indeed, they are very much linked with inner weather. My prayer becomes that great phrase of King Lear, "Sweeten my imagination," which means waiting for the return of light. Whenever I am in touch with love, with the giving self, with the goodness of people—even in darkness—then faith makes sense. It remains unsure to the Thomas-like me who stands outside. It becomes sure to the me who stands inside the circle and seeks to live its vision.

Only in that way can I give a full answer to that teacher's urgent question about being *sure* there is life after death. It is neither yes nor no. It depends on where you are, or on how you are. A sure yes at times. An unsure yes at times. But the yes of faith wins. It sounds a deeper music. It stems from a larger freedom of heart. It gives rise to a more generous living. Even though the storms are real when they come, it can survive those storms of being unsure. I can navigate through the fog without undue panic.

Just as the Magi did not always see the star, so unsureness is a common reality for everyone at times. Many people sit uneasy with official clarities, even if they seldom voice their doubts. One woman friend of mine describes herself as a bit of a Buddhist in her Christianity, in that she prefers not to be too clear about God. There is Someone she meets in meditation, but he or she has no face and sometimes seems more an Absence than a Presence. This same friend stayed away from the sacraments for years, in part, because she felt their language was too definite for her. She remained an honest questioner, never quite at home with official religion and its usual expressions. There are many like her who have at least temporary periods of healthy unease with what she calls the cocksure language of the church. The mystery of God is more strange by far than the many unambiguous words pronounced from altars on Sunday.

How then, in practice, can we cope wisely with the dark? St. Ignatius Loyola offered a few classical suggestions in his *Spiritual Exercises*, when he spoke of surviving through times of desolation. His advice could be boiled down to three maxims.

1. Don't change your course in the dark.
2. Push in the opposite direction of your negative moods.
3. Trust that this empty time will not last.

And this translates perfectly into the story of the Magi.

1. They kept going, even when the journey seemed a madcap quest, and when they lost the clarity of their initial light.

2. When the star was not guiding them, they looked for help. In other words, they acted against any inclination to abandon the adventure.

3. Their perseverance was rewarded by the return of the star, so that they emerged from confusion into clarity again.

Viewed in this way, darkness can be a friend of faith. The absence of steady light is inevitable on any journey of meaning. Indeed, it forces us to admit that the strange experience of faith is a unique mixture of fragility and strength, of doubt and certitude.

CHAPTER FOUR

ASKING QUESTIONS: A DIALOGUE

For such a short story, Matthew's account of the Magi mentions many occasions of questioning. The Magi arrive in Jerusalem and ask, "Where is the infant king of the Jews?" Next, Herod asks his group of experts, "Where is the Christ to be born?" and he later interrogates the Magi as to the "exact date on which the star had appeared."

To ask questions is a basic human activity. It starts with a child's cascade of daily inquiries and continues in different and deeper ways through life.

A faith without questions may have existed serenely in simpler cultures but today it is almost unthinkable. There are many basic questions about religion today, and it is a time of more questions than answers. To do justice to them requires the right wavelength, a reverence that goes beyond mere argument.

Marriage Preparation

Richard and Marian were former students of mine and I was delighted when they asked me to perform their marriage. When we met to plan the ceremony, all went well until we ran into the question of communion. I knew Marian to be a firm believer and weekly communicant, but I had never discussed religion with Richard. He seemed embarrassed by the communion question but was inclined to say yes. When he told me that he had been out of touch with church practice for several years, I suggested that to come to a good decision over communion might need more time than this quick conversation, which was inevitably focused on the details of the ceremony. I proposed a longer talk, saying that it might be one of the few moments in his life when he had the opportunity to take stock of his religious situation.

Without any hesitation, Richard agreed to meet with me, saying that the whole area of his faith had been dormant for years. So we met for what turned out to be a most enjoyable conversation, which left both of us feeling grateful. Indeed, our exchanges seemed so worthwhile that I wrote them down and developed the text as a wedding gift for both of them. Here is a version of our communion dialogue.

M.P.G.:   Tell me something about your faith story, about what God meant for you at any time, or about how it changed.

Richard: That's easy enough. I think I believed in God without difficulty until about thirteen or fourteen, and then it very simply collapsed. Fairly quickly in fact. I could not reconcile the idea of God creating the world with all the new ideas I was picking up from science.

M.P.G.:   So it was an intellectual crisis of a kind?

Richard: Yes, insofar as a young teenager can have an intellectual crisis. It was not a painful crisis really. I just stopped believing in God the way I had been brought up to do.

M.P.G.:   How did your faith crisis come about? Did anything in

	particular happen to trigger your doubts?
Richard:	It was mainly in my own thoughts. I didn't express it very much, except in religion class and there it got me into trouble. At least the teacher responded to my questions with a certain amount of sarcasm. So I shut up.
M.P.G.:	The questions were shot down. Were you hurt by that?
Richard:	Oh, sure. But I don't think that was the key to my not believing. I think I just gave up trying to find answers and decided the whole faith thing was for children.
M.P.G.:	Like Santa Claus. Something you grow out of. Something you find out was a fiction for small kids.
Richard:	Exactly, and with as little sense of pain as about Santa Claus.
M.P.G.:	Was there no difficulty at home, if you stopped going to Mass for instance?
Richard:	I didn't stop immediately. I gradually went less and less. Most of my peers were doing the same. Besides, my parents weren't pushy about practice, unlike some of the others.
M.P.G.:	So it was mainly internal. God became incredible because of science. I take it you stopped any personal prayer.
Richard:	That disappeared in time. In fact, the whole religion thing went blank for me until last week. I sometimes had discussions with friends but they were just arguments on the surface. Nothing disturbed my blankness, my absence of questions, until the issue of communion at the wedding came up.
M.P.G.:	I'm glad we didn't gloss over that. I think it's important to look for what might be the right or honest decision there. It sounds to me as if your faith needle got stuck fairly early in life and hasn't had a chance to move since. You've had no moments when you thought of re-examining the God question for yourself?

Richard: Not really. Someone like you—a priest and all—might not realize how rare it is to have the right wavelength to raise these questions.

M.P.G.:   Perhaps we have it now.

Richard: I think we have. What do you think about my story, as you called it?

M.P.G.:   Perhaps a mixture of the unusual and the usual. I think it's usual for people of your generation to go fairly blank on God. It's more unusual to do so without pain, and so early, and over something that could have been answered.

Richard: How would you answer it now?

M.P.G.:   Partly I'd say that now is different than then. At twenty-three, you're rather different in yourself than what you were at fourteen. I think you're able to approach the whole issue of faith more maturely. It's a personal question, which is not to say that it simply depends on what you feel. I mean, it's a question that involves how you see your life. To believe in God is a personal business, not just a matter of proving a First Cause for the universe. It sounds as if you got caught in that second agenda out of the sheer thrill of learning to think for yourself. Was science very exciting for you then?

Richard: Engrossing. Fascinating. A whole new world.

M.P.G.:   It seemed to explain everything.

Richard: It did then.

M.P.G.:   And now?

Richard: It's not the same. It's important, but there are other things.

M.P.G.:   Like...?

Richard: Like falling in love and getting married.

M.P.G.:   A whole new world—to quote you! And it changes the wavelength we were talking about.

Richard: How do you mean?

M.P.G.:   I mean that you are able to wonder about faith in a much richer way now. The only God you could believe in or not believe in at fourteen was an Explanation of the World, a kind of theorem. But the only God worth believing is in Someone utterly different from that: what the Old Testament calls the God of Abraham, of Isaac, of Jacob. In other words, a God of persons. Or what the New Testament calls the God who is love. You're now mature enough for that vocabulary and can understand God in a loving personal relationship. Because you have experienced it in your own way with Marian. Doesn't that make a big difference?

Richard: It's the biggest thing that has ever happened to me. I suppose it must change the way I think about everything.

M.P.G.: Including God?

Richard: I hadn't really been thinking about God until this conversation. All these years it was a no-go area, not in the sense of anything forbidden or rejected, but simply dead, something to be avoided.

M.P.G.: Did you believe you had solved the question of God at fourteen? In the negative, I mean.

Richard: Not really. I stopped wondering about it. I shelved it as impossible, and I was able to live without God, quite easily in fact.

M.P.G.: And now? Even as we talk?

Richard: It might become real again, or in a new way. I'm surprised at how I'm feeling. Perhaps I'm closer to faith than I thought.

M.P.G.: In what way, would you say?

Richard: A bit like you said. I know more about life than I did at fourteen. I'm less cerebral now. I believe in the personal now and in the possibility of love. If there is a God, I can't think of God as just some cold explanation of everything.

M.P.G.: Go on. God will be found as...

Richard: A person you might love.

M.P.G.:   Or a person who might love you. Perhaps that comes first.

Richard: Why do you say that? I was always taught that you had to love God.

M.P.G.:   There is something crucial we haven't touched on yet. Or, more accurately, someone. Can you guess?

Richard: Jesus Christ, I suppose.

M.P.G.:   Exactly. What, if anything, does he mean to you?

Richard: I'm vague on that. I have a jumble of pictures in my head, like an art gallery! But I don't know what it adds up to: just old photos, or dim memories.

M.P.G.:   Memories of what?

Richard: Childhood, I suppose. When I used to pray to Jesus. When he was a kind of friend.

M.P.G.:   You had a sense of Jesus as friend before that crisis broke at fourteen. Can you remember your first communion?

Richard: Clearly. At least the externals of the day, dressing up in white and all that.

M.P.G.:   And communion itself. Did it mean much to you?

Richard: It was important in some way I can't explain, in a way I've lost touch with now. It was like having a special friend. I would never be alone. But I can't return to that now. It's too simple.

M.P.G.:   Yes and no. You've grown up. The images of childhood won't meet your needs now. But what you glimpsed at your first communion could have its truth still: Jesus as a friend who comes. Or as I was saying, a God who loves you. It may sound too simple but it's at the heart of any personal faith. Otherwise you end up with a non-Christian god. You can't pray to an Ultimate Explanation. You don't receive the First Cause in communion.

Richard: What do *you* believe you receive in communion?

M.P.G.:   What Jesus gave at his last supper. From all the gospel
           accounts of that meal, it was an evening when Jesus
           wanted to give of himself totally. A kind of farewell
           gift. He spoke of sharing his own peace and joy with
           his disciples; he promised to send them his Spirit to be
           within them; he gave them a new command—to love
           as he had loved them, as he had symbolized for them
           by washing their feet. As if to crown all this sharing, he
           took bread and wine and said...perhaps you remember
           the words yourself?

Richard: This is my body. This is my blood.

M.P.G.:   Yes, but there is more. Other words that make all the
           difference, I think.

Richard: I don't remember any more. Just the claim that this
           bread was his body, which is something I've found im-
           possible to believe.

M.P.G.:   The second half can make it more possible to believe.
           Jesus breaks the bread and gives it to them saying,
           "This is my body which will be given up for you." The
           breaking looks forward to the next day and the cross.
           The whole purpose of his self-giving is for others. You
           can't appreciate communion unless you see how it is
           related to all the self-giving by Jesus at that last supper,
           and indeed in his whole life.

Richard: You mean the communion bread is a symbol of self
           giving rather than what people call the "real pres-
           ence"?

M.P.G.:   We're getting into deep water there. No, I would not
           see them as alternatives. Communion is both the pres-
           ence of Jesus and a symbol of what he was to do the
           next day. There is no greater love, he said, than to lay
           down your life for your friends. In this spirit he gave
           himself in bread and wine at the supper just as he was
           going to do on the cross. And of course he added, "Do

this in memory of me." What "this" are we to "do,"
would you think?

Richard: Say these words. Say Mass. Give communion.

M.P.G.: Any other possibility that you see?

Richard: I don't know. Perhaps imitate what you were stressing
there, his whole gesture of self-giving.

M.P.G.: Exactly. If we forget that central gesture of love, we
miss the core of that last supper. We reduce it to ritual,
or make it seem like magic. If we just perform his ac-
tions without trying to live his way, we make the eucharist a hollow pietism. And I'm afraid that often happens.

So where does all this leave you? We've covered a
lot of ground. Perhaps too much. We started off talking
about faith itself, and that led to the question of communion. From there we got into the need to live the
surrender of Jesus, and now we're wondering how our
celebration of Mass can do justice to the mystery of the
last supper. Where are we, do you think?

Richard: I'm learning a lot, although I'm a bit lost too. It's all
very interesting. More than interesting, it's opening my
eyes to things. I don't know if I can take it all in just
yet, or if I can believe it all. But it certainly changes the
picture of faith that I had, or the sense of communion
that I was starting from.

M.P.G.: Describe the differences a bit. What has come into focus for you as we've been talking?

Richard: A few good things. Perhaps the most important would
be a challenge to my old agenda about God. I was
probably a bit childish in throwing God out just because I could not square God's existence with my teen-
age enthusiasm over science. I see that I might be more
ripe for exploring faith now because it's more a personal thing than an objective thing. I've grown through

	new experiences in my own life, most of all the experience of love. So I can approach the question of God differently now.
M.P.G.:	What's the main change in approach there?
Richard:	Probably that I should not expect a clear proof for God and that I should not abandon the search, because that kind of certainty is impossible.
M.P.G.:	And more positively...?
Richard:	That's harder to pinpoint. If there is a God, my relationship would be more personal. I suppose that's where Christ would come into the picture.
M.P.G.:	And does he for you now?
Richard:	I can't say. I need time to let all this sink in a bit more. You've no idea how new all this is for me. These are things I haven't thought about ever before.
M.P.G.:	If you remain unsure about Christ and faith in him, can you decide to receive communion? That, after all, was our starting point.
Richard:	It's not so much that I remain unsure. It's that I'd have to ponder it a bit. I'd certainly like to be able to receive communion. I liked how you were explaining it as Christ's gift of himself at that last supper, and how it summarized all he stood for. What do you think I should do?
M.P.G.:	I'd trust your own feeling—that you need time to think, space to let all this sink in. Except I'd open it into the possibility of prayer.
Richard:	I should say some prayers?
M.P.G.:	That's not what I said. If, as you say, you give time to wondering where you are in all this, that could become a reaching out to God and that's what prayer is.
Richard:	How could that happen? I haven't prayed for years.
M.P.G.:	I'm not sure what would help you most. Could it be that you're not alone in all this? Could you pause and listen in quiet for the invitation of the Spirit? I believe

that the Spirit of God is within you. Or you might find that Scripture is a road to prayer. You might take one of the communion passages and let it become personal. For instance, where Jesus says "I am the bread of life; no one who comes to me shall ever be hungry." If Jesus is God, then those words are spoken for you as much as for his first listeners. He's speaking about himself as meeting all your longing as well as about the gift of communion. But I can't teach you to pray. I can only encourage you to listen in your own way, and to be open to finding yourself listening to God.

Richard: That sounds a big step for me—at least from where I have been for so long.

M.P.G.: It's a step that countless thousands have taken each in his or her own way. "Seek and you will find." I think the moment is ripe. But you have to be free. Real faith is always born out of a deep freedom.

Richard: You may be right. I'll try to give it a chance these days. Perhaps the trouble before was that I was never free about religion, and never realized that it needed another kind of listening, another kind of searching.

M.P.G.: Or that God might search for you.

Richard: That would be a surprise, but let's see over the next while—some surprises do happen.

CHAPTER FIVE

TRAVELING TOGETHER: COMMUNITY

It is always assumed that there were three Magi, but in fact the gospel does not say this. It simply mentions three gifts, and on the basis of this, tradition has usually supposed three givers of those gifts. Sometimes the artists have shown more than three—up to twelve—but gradually it became a convention to depict them as one elderly man, one younger man, and one non-white.

What is clear from the text is that there was more than one of them and that they traveled together. In fact there were two groups of people who recognized and welcomed Jesus at his birth: the shepherds who were from nearby, simple and caring Jewish people who did not expect anything special; the others, the Magi, were from far away, non-Jewish people who were more conscious searchers after wisdom.

Community seems to be the normal birthplace and home for faith. So we might now ask, what is the role of companionship with others on this road of searching? What is happening to our togetherness in the contemporary world and the contemporary church?

Social Changes

Once I found myself called on to help a young man. At twenty-two, he had never had steady employment, and as a result remained withdrawn and shaky in his self-confidence. Yet I knew him as a deep and interesting person. He asked me for a job reference, which I was happy to give him. We also filled out the application form together. When he was leaving, he said, "You've been very good to me." My first impulse was to reply with a conventional "Not at all," but I paused and found myself voicing a fuller truth: "I hope so, but it takes two to make goodness." In other words, we need others to awaken the goodness that is in each of us, and to bring it out into the open. We are here in this world for one another, even if it is rare to admit that basic truth openly and simply.

Paradoxically, we grow by giving. We receive by sharing. We stay alive by little dyings for the sake of another. This is true not only in daily kindnesses between people, such as a job reference (the one in question actually worked!), but in the large-scale project of healing this divided and troubled planet. Where would any of us be in our humanity without the wonder and trust born from friends, and from glimpsing their mystery and richness? Yeats's poem *The Municipal Gallery Revisited* describes him looking around at the portraits of many he had known in his life, and the poem ends, "and say my glory was I had such friends."

Such companionship is central to most people's lives. Yet there is a larger circle of traveling together, one that is crucial for faith: how we belong with one another in communities of various kinds. Of all that determines how people see their lives differently today than they did in the past, nothing has more impact than the changes in how we live together. Less than two centuries ago, most people lived in a rural rhythm. Now the world is predominantly urbanized, with vast numbers living side by side with people they do not know. Where do we truly belong any more? With whom do we find belonging? These questions no longer have easy or automatic answers. This is all the more true of the rich world, in which wealth has paid for fences, security systems, and space that isolates the private property of the self or that unit called the nuclear family. Volumes have been written about this, but the core fact is that people have lost one form of belonging together without finding any genuine alternative.

There is no point in being nostalgic about those older community supports or in dreaming that they could possibly return. A certain world is dead forever. What is vital is to recognize the price we have paid in human terms for our modernity. The shift from a society of belonging to a society of anonymity has changed how we image our humanity. One result is that faith has become something private, even for many believers, as well as marginal as a force within Western culture. Indeed this crisis of faith today is largely a by-product of how we live together, or rather how we do not live together. A death of community lies at the origin of much so-called unbelief or alienation from church or loss of a sense of the spiritual. Remembering the Magi plot again, if Herod can kill belonging or community, he may not need to kill Jesus.

A hunger for new community is one of the hallmarks of our time. Sometimes that hope lies dormant, suppressed by our urban addictions to spending, distractions, entertainment, novelty, and so on. But this need for community has become an urgent quest for many who awaken to the ravages of Herod's rule. They sense that being a Christian cannot be a solitary journey, that faith has never flourished except where community exists in one form or another. If the older languages of belonging in both society and church have collapsed, then new ways of traveling the road together must be found.

It is one of the most exciting aspects of church life today that community is being rediscovered with rich variety and in many places. Perhaps of all the faith dimensions suggested by the Magi story, this traveling together has become the most crucial in today's world. There are other important strands such as imagination, social alertness, prayerfulness, generosity, or commitment, but without a living community, faith is in danger of remaining merely private, and therefore stunted. In the image of the sower parable, where faith lacks social roots, it may wither under the scorching sun (Matthew 13:6).

Community of Brokenness

In this light I offer here a few accounts of how the hunger for community has been met in different ways. My first example of how traveling together can be life-giving comes from my contacts over a few years with Narcotics Anonymous, or N.A. Indeed this privileged experience with ex-addicts has forced me to see the issues more starkly and to admit less grudgingly my own need for community, something that by temperament I tend to neglect. Here is what I wrote after returning from an N.A. retreat. I present it untouched in order to give a sense of my gratitude for these friends and to convey something of the unique community into which they welcomed me.

It's not often that I come home after midnight and have the urge to write instead of going to bed. But it happened tonight. Not for the first time I find myself both stunned and refreshed by the sheer honesty of humanity that I find in N.A. They are all young people who have hit bottom through drugs. All of them remain fragile inside, vulnerable from their experience, haunted by memories and guilt. But my overall sense of them is one of resurrection, of new life. Out of darkness and evil and "shit," as they say, is born feelowship (that started as a typing error but let it stand)—it is a fellowship of shared feelings with nothing soft about it.

There is something of transparent authority about people who have come through so much suffering. It is hard to identify or describe. Is it a kind of wisdom born of woundedness? Or a courage of down-to-earthness? Or an absence of the usual games, masks, and defenses of us less broken ones? It may seem strange that being broken can lead to such depth and life. Perhaps because they were dangerously hooked on an illusion, they can see through other surface games that distract people from their real selves. The rest of us avoid humbling experiences unless they are forced upon us. Some moments leave us exposed or ashamed, but if we raise our shields fast enough, nobody will notice, and then we can forget. We are born evaders of weakness. We are polished pretenders in our pride. We are experts in dodging our essential poverty and therefore the more costly avenues of grace appear to be unnatural to us.

What I witnessed with N.A. cuts through all that nonsense—and it is nonsense, literally, *non-sense*. These people are in touch with their hungers because they are in touch with their hurts. They have stepped outside the conspiracy of half-truth or untruth that so often dominates our "normality"—to the extent that we do not know the lives we live. Because they have hit rock bottom but have come through, there is a directness in their emotions and an openness about their need for one another. Their addiction was an experience of profound isolation but they have emerged from it through the discovery of community. In this way they have seen through one of the key heresies of our culture, namely, that standing on one's own feet is the only way to live, and that dependence on others is some kind of weakness or immaturity. When they abandoned this inherited stance of isolation, they found the healing space that is community, solidarity, friendship, support. They know now how crazy it was, and is, to think that we can dispense with sharing the road with others. In our world, individualism presents itself as the unquestioned path, but in fact it is a blinkered version, and another kind of addiction.

This addiction to the private self has come home to me in my other rather different world of university. Discussing literature in a tutorial group, students assume that "character" is *the* vital question in novels or plays. They have been brought up on a diet of personal consciousness (as I was a generation back). But they seldom see through the subjectivism in this. Nor do they suspect that they could be victims of a culture that makes the self into an idol or that keeps their morality stuck on the childish level of "If it feels OK, do it."

Recently, I remarked that for the majority of the human race these assumptions about the self do not hold, that in the Third World a sense of community is stronger than this ferocious sense of the individual. I was not claiming that there is no egoism in the barrios of Latin America—far from it—but that individuals there do not have the same inflated sense of their own importance nor suffer from the radical aloneness imposed on people by our Western life patterns. In similar fashion, the modern university often leaves its students disillusioned. Where they had hoped for wisdom and friendship, often they encounter only cleverness and competition. Thus the university becomes a microcosm of the First World as a whole. Yet with all its advantages, it ends up condemning people to situations of non-relationship, and this imposed solitude can in turn stifle their sense of God.

By contrast, the discovery by many friends in N.A., born from tragedy and pain, is that it is impossible to survive without community. In this respect, what they and other groups are doing is counter-cultural. They are seeking something that is too basic to be put on sale in Herod's supermarket. In those N.A. members, I see the gospel's "poverty of spirit" in so many forms: in the joy of having come through the horrors and found friends who know the road; in honesty over failure; in the absence of silly pride and in the presence of a good-humored acceptance of one another; and above all, in the willingness to admit hurt and then to care for one another as they travel the road together.

Faith Friends

I have chosen to give pride of place to the N.A. community experience, because it seems a powerful and transparent example of a basic point, namely, that any Magi-like search for wisdom is bound to remain weak unless it finds the unique strength that lies in community. Thus, within the anonymity that is modern socie-

ty, the contemporary church is learning to create gatherings of believers, people who come together to support one another in
searching for the gospel vision now.

For instance, it has been a special pleasure for me to be involved in a "faith friends" group of young adults in one of the
more deprived areas of our city. The group first gathered in late
September and then met weekly until about April, when they
went out in pairs to share what they had found with children preparing for confirmation. Although everyone knew from the outset
that the group would eventually serve this purpose with the "confirmation kids," practically no mention of this arose until about
March. Instead, all these months were spent in an unpredictable
adventure of human and spiritual discovery, where the members
themselves set the agenda.

Each week, with help from the priest leading the program, they
would decide on a topic for the following Monday. It could be
anything, from the image of the local town as a problem area to
the experience of being an unmarried parent, from drawing one's
image of God and explaining it, to reflecting together on what
blocks us from being our real selves with others. It was exciting to
watch the development of warmth and trust among the group,
predominantly male in fact, and drawn from such a tough area.
The shy ones turned out to be not so shy after all. The "hard" ones
turned out to be imaginative and "soft." In religious terms, the
non-practicing and unbelieving ones turned out to have deep
hungers and real questions.

At some stage before Christmas, the group started to end each
evening with an exercise in guided silent meditation. It was a total novelty for most of those present and proved a marvelous
breakthrough for them. Lasting about twenty minutes, it usually
involved some stillness exercise leading into a fantasy, and finished with a prayer. After Christmas the discussion topics tended
to be more explicitly religious: Bible, church, Mass, prayer, the
Holy Spirit, and so on. By this stage such an excellent spirit had
been built up within the group that people who would not nor-

mally talk about spiritual issues found themselves free to speak their questions and voice their inner selves.

I recall with relish the good humor with which one man reported that he had been praying without knowing it! He described how, as a result of the capacity for quiet time learned from the periods of group meditation, he found himself staring out of the window at the rain for a long time, but instead of it being a waste of time or an empty dream, it was a moment of attentive wonder, with a sense of God behind it all.

The success of this group was that it opened up new levels of expression for people who had been limited by a narrow vocabulary for their humanity and their faith. The sheer happiness of the weekly meetings was a great experience of community and of mutual enjoyment. Looking back at the evolution of trust in the group, it seems proof of the validity of starting with people's lived realities if we are to arrive at a genuine faith language for today. First, we had established a basis of friendship and of human sharing. Then, we became more ambitious and personal in the topics we took for reflection. Next, we opened a door to an experience of interiority through the exercises in meditative quiet. This led to a local version of "theology from below," a way of understanding issues of faith as arising from human experience. This rooting of our reflections in life was a slower road for learning, but a much more fruitful one than beginning with a discussion of formal doctrines.

Moreover, this participation in that Faith Friends group brought about in me something of a conversion to community. I saw again why, in modern pastoral thinking, so much stress is put on small communities as key places for growth in faith. Trust and truth together seem rare in our urban societies. But if such basic human hungers are trivialized and starved, they do not disappear. Rather, they emerge readily and eagerly whenever real nourishment is available. It was certainly exciting to witness those young adults discovering and creating a weekly oasis of community within our high-rise jungle of apartments.

Marriage and Celibacy

At the opposite end of the social scale, I have also been chaplain for several years to a group of married couples belonging to the Teams of Our Lady. This international body, which originated in France just before the Second World War, now exists as a Catholic movement of couples throughout the world. A team is a small community, usually up to seven couples, who meet monthly with a chaplain. Following the insights of the movement's founder, Henri Caffarel, the focus is on a spirituality rooted in the experience of married love. He found that many couples were leading parallel lives of private religious duties, without ever voicing their faith to one another. The team's way of life stresses a spiritual journey that is discussed and shared.

Our monthly meetings are held in the homes of each family in turn and begin with a meal, the preparation of which is shared by all. After this pleasant start, the remainder of the meeting is given to listening to one another in some depth on the important happenings of each family as well as on the various commitments of our team spirituality: daily personal prayer, reading of Scripture, a monthly "sit-down" or special listening to one's spouse, and some rule of life or growth point that each individual chooses for herself or himself. Later on, we have some time of guided silent prayer, which leads to a sharing of prayer by everyone. The last part of the evening is devoted to the topic, usually a religious book, that we study chapter by chapter, pooling and discussing our responses with one another. Thus a fair bit of ground was covered in the three or so hours of the monthly meeting.

Describing the Teams in this way may be necessary for those who do not know the movement, but it totally fails to capture its spirit as a community experience. One member of our team came close when he said, "I don't think I would still be a Catholic without the Teams." He felt that under all the pressures of modern life, he would have lost his spiritual bearings had it not been for two gifts found through the movement: the companionship with other couples and the stimulus to growth in faith.

The Team that I was with had five couples of middle-class background, mostly with children in their teens or older. This too was a genuine experience of community, less dramatic and less intense than Narcotics Anonymous or the Faith Friends, but equally real in its slower rhythm of traveling together through the years.

The couples found it a source of great support in times of tension as well as in the dry and routine times of life. Together we have carried one another through moments of serious illness and bereavement, and through anxiety about children and their decisions. At times, we have shared with one another our struggles and personal burdens, and this has often proved a unique safety net in periods of darkness. We have also celebrated moments of success and joy. What now seems impressive, looking back on twelve years together, is that each couple has been able to find nourishment through the community of the team. It is one more verification of the fruitfulness of such anchors in today's society. Without them many people suffer from a malnutrition of both humanity and faith.

For me, involvement with the Teams brought insights into both marriage and celibacy that I might not have reached otherwise. I heard couples describe the shock experienced during the first years of marriage as two previously independent selves had to adjust first to one another, then to children, and later to all the ups and downs of family life. And I began to wonder whether the demands of marriage were not harder to live with than the demands of priesthood. Both callings are meant to lead to freedom for love, but my fear is that priesthood can more easily side step the challenge and thus fall short of the real reason for celibacy. As a priest, I can function quite caringly behind the armor of a role, but without any lasting erosion of my egoism or fundamental conversion of heart.

No doubt a similar evasion is possible within marriage. Yet watching the tough yet happy letting go that marks the lives of married friends, I feel challenged about the quality of my love and about the quality of my nourishing of that love in the silence of prayer. Their sacrifices, lived day in, day out, remind me of the call at the core of celibacy, if it is to be fulfilled and happy. It is a call to some contemplative space where the heart can learn from God. The trouble is that I can shirk entering that space without anyone knowing, whereas if my married friends shirk their family relationships, their doing so is much more evident to all concerned.

Celibacy becomes dangerous, I think, when it lacks prayerful listening, for then it loses touch with its main justification, which is mystical. Years ago I used to be more content with a functional view of celibacy—the claim that without family commitments, I can be free for people. But both my experience of myself and this contact with married friends have convinced me that the value of celibacy lies beyond this practical sphere. Absence of sexual intimacy, just for the sake of pastoral activity, would be too high a price to pay. Rather it must be "for the Kingdom," as the gospel says, in the sense of sharing in the heart of Christ. Only by entering that alternative story, with its costs and its fullfilments, can one be liberated to care for people. Perhaps, therefore, celibacy should not be linked to priesthood as an obligation. But that is not the issue here. Our theme is how faith needs traveling together of various kinds, regardless of whether people are married or celibate. Especially today, faith without community seems a contradiction, an unnecessary handicap to our hopes.

Variety of Community

There are of course many other examples of the power of community in fostering faith. I think of the attraction of Taizé, the ecumenical monastery in southern France, where thousands of young people converge each summer to find spiritual nourishment and the experience of community. They share their hopes, and support one another in all sorts of ways, from dishwashing to silence. Above all, they learn that life need not be such an egoist prison, and that the cries of the world in need require them to build themselves into living communities.

I was blessed to see yet another face of community in Latin America. It is the secret of that continent, and of its liberation spirituality, that its people have discovered a joy in communities built "from below." On any given evening one can know that thousands of people are gathering in groups of faith, centered on the Bible, where they listen to their realities and discern their way of life. Just from sitting in on some of these gatherings, I learned that justice must begin with such basics as water supplies or the collection of rubbish. Where the poor are deprived of these ordinary needs, the communities of faith struggle to bring about change in the spirit of the gospel. It was one of the joys of my stay in Latin America to experience Sunday eucharist within vibrant communities of poor people. They took their time and were not shy in sharing their response to the Scriptures. They welcomed strangers and were generous to any in need. They sang with energy and prayed with devotion. Most of all, they communicated a confidence in their own kind of church. This was where their strength lay, where their hopes were rooted, where their faith in God found central expression.

Finally, what of my own experience of living as a religious in community for nearly thirty years? Jesuits are not known for community. We put less stress on it than other religious families. Even from the historical fact, so strange at the time of our foundation, that we do not pray the breviary in common, a certain individualism can become the norm. But for me, community has come to be more and more important with the years, especially since I have lived mainly in small communities with students in formation. There was always considerable interaction and mutual support, from sharing the cooking to a commitment to prayerful listening to each person, from being there for each other in dull everyday events to the more difficult task of facing the tensions among us.

Probably my happiest experience has been to find myself surprisingly cared for. People challenged me over my excessive tiredness; they listened to my struggles and supported me in all sorts of ways; they offered a friendship that never invaded my basic privacy, and an encouragement for my gifts that never forgot to tease my silly obsessions. For me, another important experience of religious community has to do with obedience. It has been good to know that decisions reached by superiors were rooted in a care for me and for others, and in a prayerful search for what is best. It was consoling to be part of that process and to be listened to in a genuine way.

Strange to say, perhaps my deepest experiences of Jesuit community have been of forgiveness, where fellow Jesuits accepted me in my difficult moods and thereby mirrored to me the compassion of God. It could be something as simple as being able to express anger without guilt, because the others accepted my feelings as a natural part of me.

As I was writing this chapter on community, I had a visit from an old friend who was about to leave for some years in Africa. Since it would be years before we saw each other again, I found myself saying to him, "I hope you find friends there who can meet you in your depths. More than that, I hope you can find others who might share a project, a vision, a search of some kind. Like the Magi." Perhaps that is the difference between the need for friendship and the need for community. Community is bigger, not only in numbers but because it builds on a shared meaning and a shared goal. In this sense being a Christian is to belong with others, and the rediscovery of community—in exciting variety—is one of the truly consoling signs of faith today.

CHAPTER SIX

THE HEROD PLOT

I have sometimes tested the memory of people about the Magi story, inviting them to recall whatever details they could. Most people seemed to remember the star and the gifts but they often needed some prompting before mentioning what gets relatively a good deal of space in St. Matthew. "Does this story have a villain?" I would ask. And only then would the Herod subplot come back to them.

It is striking that each of the infancy stories in the gospel contains some note of hostility or conflict. The annunciation at first causes Mary to be deeply disturbed. Her *magnificat* hymn of praise is also a prophecy against the rich and powerful. Months later, the inn is shut against a pregnant woman. Later still, Simeon, at the very moment of his joyful recognition of the Messiah, adds that Jesus will be rejected and that Mary's soul will be pierced by a sword.

Thus these stories, which most of us encounter as children, have an adult edge to them as well. The entry of Jesus into history includes division and opposition. There are those who receive him—the shepherds and Simeon and Anna and the Magi—and those who close the door on him or even try to kill him, like Herod.

Herod's main reason for wanting to be rid of Jesus was that he could not tolerate another king. It is a tale of two kinds of kingship. It is also a story of pretense, where the powerful one appears to be religious in order to control the situation. "When you have found him, let me know, so that I too may go and do him homage."

Where is Herod now? He is alive and well and living in our many systems of oppression, assuming various disguises to continue his old deceptions in new ways.

The Worlds of Clare and Eliseo

"Are we all sucked into it, sooner or later, this rat race? Is there any hope of escaping its clutches?" I remember a sunny afternoon in a park when Clare poured out her reactions to the strange world around her. She was spending the summer as a trainee social worker in a big city and running into plenty of reality. In many ways she had foreseen those tough realities and was ready for them: the desperation of a single mother, alone with an infant and unable to find friends; the suicidal depression of an ex-prisoner; the tensions of having to take a child away from two drug-addict parents; the demanding old man who reported her bad manners to the office. To live with these situations day by day was far from easy, but something else was disturbing Clare.

Was it a sense of impotence before the accumulation of problems in this city? Was it the contrast between this underside of society and other parts of the city where wealth was habitually on display? Was it the seemingly cold professionalism that she noticed in older social workers, as if they had to harden themselves to cope with it all? All these things pressed in on Clare, but the key to her unrest lay elsewhere. "It's as if something sick is in control; a kind of uncaring saturates this place. But there must be something else, mustn't there? Where can God be in all this?"

Faced with Clare's questions, my temptation was to be too positive too quickly. It would have been easy to say, and not untrue, that God was there in the care that Clare was bringing to people. But her question stemmed from a wider sense of trouble. She had glimpsed, as it were, a system of egoism enthroned in this city, something that was larger than any of the victims she visited in her work. This system, like a cynical Herod, was able to shrug off any quick-fix gestures of individual kindness. (What harm are these do-gooders, as long as I run the show?) Out of her personal experience, Clare was sensing the futility of any merely personal responses if Herod continues to rule the kingdom.

Against this memory of life in a first world city, I recall a contrasting response from Paraguay. Once again it concerns a young person of social conscience and high ideals. But in Latin America the Herod situation is different, and perhaps it is easier to see one's way in a world of more obvious oppression. Eliseo was a seminarian I met in Asuncion in 1987, while General Stroessner was still dictator, as he had been since 1954. Together with his fellow students, Eliseo planned a special Stations of the Cross for the Monday of holy week, which was to include a procession in the streets near the national seminary.

Nothing could be more normal for Latin America. But the students announced that this commemoration of the passion of Christ would be in solidarity with peasant leaders evicted from their land and imprisoned without trial. These men had been agitating for land reform in a country where a small minority of the rich holds nearly all the best land. Clearly, such a protest was liable to bring down the wrath of the authorities. Besides, there was a history of tension between church and regime over justice for Paraguay's many impoverished farmers.

Less than a year before, when some peasants had been killed, the bishops took the unprecedented step of calling out the priests and religious in the capital for a silent procession carrying the Virgin of Ka'akupe. The police were powerless to intervene, because although they might easily attack church leaders, it would be unthinkable to insult Paraguay's most famous statue. Possibly in response to this challenge, General Stroessner's Christmas message for 1986 stressed the need to distinguish between "good" and "bad" priests. Good priests were those who served the spiritual needs of people, but bad priests "used religion to interfere with society, disturbing people with leftist notions of justice, and being disobedient to the pope." (It is worth remarking that the same pope on his visit to Paraguay in May 1988 proved himself to be a "bad priest": his strong speeches on human rights were an acute embarrassment to Stroessner and may have helped drive the dictator from office several months later.)

I mention all this to give some background for the story of Eliseo. His world of social conflict and of religious culture would differ

enormously from that confronted by Clare. His response to his situation also had a quite different tone. Clare felt confused, isolated,
and burdened by a sense of helplessness, but Eliseo was confi-
dently and happily rooted in a community of struggle larger than
himself. As part of a Christian community, he took part in that
gesture of solidarity with the prisoners.

Persecuted in the Cause of Right

That Monday afternoon, the procession of students and staff of
the seminary got less than fifty yards outside the gates when it
was attacked by police in riot gear. The peasant-made bare cross
was broken, its crown of thorns thrown to the ground. About thirty
students were injured, two seriously. Later that same day, Eliseo
told me that as the batons fell on him, his pain gave way to anger:
he wanted to scream out insults at the police. Then across his
mind flashed a scene from the film *Gandhi* where the central figure stood with dignity as police rods crashed down on him, and
Eliseo found himself thinking, "If he could do it for his people, I
can do it for mine and for Christ." At that moment he sensed
great peace in himself, in spite of the pain of the blows. The group
had been beaten back behind the gates of the seminary. In the
scuffles one of the police had lost his helmet and it now lay beside
Eliseo. He could easily have kept it as a battle trophy but another
spirit was at work. The Stations continued within the seminary
grounds, with the police lined up only yards away at the entrance. As the prayers ended. Eliseo went forward to return the
helmet to its owner, the only one without a helmet. It was roughly
received, without even a word of thanks.

This gesture, incomprehensible to that police officer, sums up
the spirit that moves many Latin American Christians in the face
of their many Herods. On that continent it is still possible to confront Herod in a gospel spirit and to hope to win. It is possible to
have a sense of history in its slow making. By contrast, the richer
worlds of the West and the North seem spiritually stagnant, ruled
by a hidden and more dehumanizing Herod. It is harder for Clare

a difference than for Eliseo. In his world, faith is
...y alive; in hers it has become a largely private
...es Herod a more subtle victory and a more dan-
...Where a merely personalist model of faith pre-
...Christian project of the Kingdom is cramped as in
a straightjacket.

Moaning vs. Critique

New hope is expressed in other parts of this book, even for the
more secularized and wealthy parts of our planet. But before
Clare could set out on that more positive search, negative discernment had to be done. As Thomas Hardy once wrote, "If way to
the better there be, it entails a full look at the worst." This task of
seeing through the nonsense that surrounds us need not be a depressing business. What is depressing is to be a confused victim
of forces that are not recognized. What is liberating is to grasp the
nettle of critique as opposed to merely moaning. Moaning means
simply complaining about "this evil world." But critique means
taking a hard and discerning look at the ways our so-called common sense is shaped. It means identifying the pressures that hold
sway in our world. It means learning that the message of King
Herod, the one in power, is not to be trusted. An arch deceiver,
his message seems attractive, friendly, interested in finding the
baby king. But in fact he is plotting murder. Only when we see
Herod clearly for what he is can we hope to find our true way
home.

Putting this more personally, my visits to Latin America con-
firmed a hunch that had been with me for some years: many of
my assumptions about faith were seriously distorted by my upbringing. It was like that moment in St. Paul when he looks back
on his formation in the law as "rubbish," as something that dam-
aged him until he found the fuller vision of Christ (Philippians
3:8).

As a child, I had no suspicions about the system surrounding
me. Even later as a student, I lived within a set of assumptions

about reality, without realizing that they were shaped in one narrow way of seeing the world. By the time I began to emerge from such ideological innocence, I had been well and truly molded by a system of wearing blinders. I can sum it up by saying that I was trained in passivity, privacy, and peace.

The first distortion, passivity, meant that authority was always right; indeed you could be punished if you questioned it in any way. It also meant that change was evil, and that people who wanted to upset the *status quo* were rebelling against God. The message I received—from nobody in particular but as a global impression—was that the established way of life was the divine order of things. God had blessed those who were comfortable and they should be grateful, while those who were poor should carry their cross with resignation.

Lopsided Upbringing

The second distortion I received—at least I have now come to see it as a distortion—was the assumption that what went on inside my consciousness was crucially important, indeed the axis of my life. This is what I mean by privacy. It was a message that came to me from many quarters. It was dominant in the approaches to literature. Most of what I was taught about prayer—from primary school up to and including early Jesuit formation—implied that this separate inner self was the key to Christian living. It was not utterly untrue, but it now seems a dangerously lopsided view. But modern culture *is* lopsided in many ways: in what it thinks of as "objective" truth, in its despising of the feminine, in its destruction of community and the environment, and so on. It all adds up to a widespread isolation and alienation in Western society, and one that became easier for me to discern from the distance of Latin America.

The third distortion concerned peace. It was as if Christianity meant peace at any price. There was no place for anger or conflict. But in Latin America, as in the case of Eliseo, conflict is inevitable. When I re-read the gospels there, I began to find that Jesus found

himself in continual conflict with the dehumanizing face of religion. Ultimately it was a confrontation that would lead to his being
killed. Previously I had often pondered and prayed the scene in
Mark's Gospel where Jesus heals the man with the withered hand.
I zoomed in on the healing of the individual and remained blind
to the fact that the episode is mainly about conflict. We are told
that "they were watching him" to see if he would dare heal on the
sabbath day. Indeed, Jesus turns the scene around, away from the
victim and puts the authorities on the spot with a probing and
ironic question: "Is it permitted on the Sabbath day to do good?"
Are they here to create or to destroy? We are told that their sitting
on the fence in silence angered him, and the scene ends with them
"discussing how to destroy him."

This simple scene is a perfect example of the "aspect blindness"
(a phrase from Wittgenstein). I tended to see the incident in purely personal terms, as a moment of healing. I ignored the fact that
most of the sentences describe tension. So it gives a whole new
tone to faith to realize the extent to which it can mean conflict
with the system—with the many ways in which Herod imposes
passivity, privacy, and a false kind of peace.

If this is true, then Herod rules today largely through the
unconscious assumptions all around us. Even though he pays lip
service to religion, it is only to a religion that stays in the sacristy
or that serves a certain "feeling good" by individuals. The net
result is that Christianity is robbed of its real power to change history. Instead, it becomes cramped into frozen forms of piety and
into unconsciousness complicity with Herod's plans. His anti-
kingdom can take many forms: it ranges from suffocating silliness
to the injustices of our divided planet. The Roman emperors provided bread and circuses to keep the masses down; perhaps the
modern emperor has his coliseum in the corner, in the shape of
television. It is like a plot to kidnap people's imagination within
the trivial and to brainwash them into an unquestioning life. No
soldiers go forth with swords, but innocents of all ages are lulled
into stupor, so that the other King is simply marginalized. Perhaps

the enemy to faith today is no longer a militant atheism but a Herod deceptively pleasant, as was that gospel figure. The dominant culture of the West does not attack faith openly: it just undermines it with other images and other priorities.

Exposing Herod in Film

Finally, I would like to draw on the clever exposure of Herod's deceptions in the film *Crimes and Misdemeanors*. Woody Allen blends comedy and seriousness with exceptional success and manages to show how faith gets cornered in today's culture. On the surface the plot is about getting away with murder, literally, but it is also a study of how conscience is stifled in the "real world." The central figure is an eye specialist called Judah Rosenthal, who is trying to end an affair without his wife finding out. But from this banal material Allen constructs a drama of two ways of seeing the world. Judah is caught between the Jewish wisdom of his childhood, where God sees everything and therefore existence has moral stability, and the "anything goes" ethic of Jack, his brother with underworld connections. One of Judah's patients is a young rabbi called Ben who, symbolically, is going blind, and who mouths kindly but bland generalities at him: he should rekindle his faith and ask his wife's forgiveness, "for without law all is darkness."

The real enemy of such old morality and the king of this society is Lester, Ben's brother and a pompous television producer, famous for junk comedies. He suppresses an unfavorable documentary on his life and work, directed by Cliff, the Woody Allen character—who is as usual a lonely and worried searcher in tough New York. The one impressive figure of wisdom is Professor Louis Levy, whom we only see on video speaking of how "we define ourselves by our choices," but in a shattering moment Allen learns that this guru has committed suicide. In this playground of images all messages are unstable and all meanings fragile. Thus, in spite of its many hilarious moments, *Crimes and Misdemeanors* is a serious exploration of what we have been describing as Herod's kingdom of deception. It is significant that at the end Judah has transformed his guilt into a television script that he outlines, somewhat tipsily, to Cliff at a wedding, and which ends, "His life is completely back to normal, back to his protected world of wealth and privilege."

Perhaps this film disturbs its audiences even more in its manner than in its content. It is not simply that the plot echoes the Herod strand of the Magi story; its mode of communication is a modern version of the dream in that gospel narrative. In its impact on its viewers this film sounds a note of warning. If it undermines complacencies and prods consciences, it does so on the level of images rather than of ideas. This is the level of dreaming (about which more will be said in a later chapter).

We are touching here on one of the roles for art within contemporary culture: it can alert the imagination to the falsities. It can, like the dream, serve as a warning system against sickness. It can mock the kingdom of Herod and leave people with a healthy suspicion about so-called normality and its charms. Although *Crimes and Misdemeanors* shows religion as ritualistic and out of touch, there is no doubt that its sympathies lie more with the ancient wisdom of faith than with the avoidance of guilt, the flouting of law, the empire of triviality that triumphs in this world where "God is a luxury I cannot afford."

It is worth adding that Allen's next move, *Alice*, went even further in the direction of religious horizons. Mia Farrow offered a great portrayal of a wealthy woman surrounded by every luxury but troubled in spirit and lacking in real human relationship. Eventually the film shows her moving toward a conversion of life, influenced by contact with the poor and with Mother Teresa in Caluctta. Although Allen remains safely on the agnostic side of religious commitment, he goes beyond mere satire of the isolation of city life; through his unique mixture of lightness and depth, he seems to be searching out older roots of community and of caring.

CHAPTER SEVEN

THE HOUSE: PROBLEMS OF CHURCH

The climax of the Magi's adventure is the moment of their discovery of Jesus. The star comes back to guide them after their interview with Herod, and it stops over the place that is the goal of their journey.

Here St. Matthew uses a phrase that might seem insignificant and yet belongs with the symbolic vocabulary so frequent in the gospels. We are told that "entering the house," they saw the child with Mary his mother. It is common knowledge that Matthew is the evangelist of the church, in the sense that he, more than the others, stresses the community of believers.

So "house" in this text may suggest the special place that is church. It can also evoke all the spaces and places where God is encountered. Here it leads us to ponder the positives and negatives of church as experienced in today's world.

A Problem Institution

I recall a student called Cormac whom I knew quite well through his university years but who spoke about his religious blockages to me only after he graduated. Fearing he might offend me, his hesitant question was this: if Jesus came back now, do you not think the church would do what the religious establishment did then—reject him and get rid of him? When I asked him to fill me in on the background of his question, he went back to his education in a Catholic secondary school and described how he came to see that institution as involved in a dishonest contradiction. The school prided itself on challenging its pupils in matters of religion, and in particular on exposing them to issues of justice and injustice. But for Cormac the real curriculum was one of cutthroat competition in all fields—academic, athletic, and social.

One episode in particular had soured his vision. Cormac was a talented athlete and would be a key figure on the football team if the school were to win the league title that year. This also made him a popular figure in the school, someone who got a lot of attention from both staff and pupils. It happened that he was badly injured early in the season and had to recuperate. So far so good. But the priest in charge of the team began to put pressure on him to return to training earlier than seemed right; Cormac resisted. It blew up into a quarrel, and the result was that Cormac decided to withdraw from the team entirely. Suddenly all the positive appreciation from the staff, religious and lay, dropped away and Cormac began to ask himself what were the real values of this Catholic school: care for people, as was always claimed officially, or a ruthless idolatry of competition, as he now experienced?

This episode gave birth to a certain suspicion that broadened into a doubt about all religious institutions. The church seemed another contradiction, officially standing for God's love, but in fact sucked into the worldly games and contaminated by them. Cormac admitted that it was rare for him to voice this root of his disenchantment. He usually contented himself with expressing the common criticisms of church—about an empty atmosphere at

Mass, about the paternalism of priests, about a predictable narrowness in church attitudes. But his main accusation went deeper than these dissatisfactions: he detected a fundamental falsity in the church, a pretense of being spiritual and caring, but a reality of being caught up in a pursuit of power and possessiveness.

Church as Human

Listening to all of Cormac's questions was frightening. It was his individual version of what Dostoevsky portrayed so terrifyingly in his parable of the Grand Inquisitor: a manipulating manager of people's religious needs who did not want any Christ to disturb his neatly functioning institution. Cormac's questioning was far from being merely intellectual; he was asking me how I could stay a priest in what he viewed as a dishonest institution. What could I say to him in response?

First of all, yes to what is true in his criticism of the church: it can become a place of falsehood and twistedness. Yes, the church in its human dimension is just that—human, and therefore, like me or Cormac, capable of goodness or of falling very short of what we are meant to be. But in case this admission of guilt seems too glib, I admit that the church gives much more scandal when it falls short than does some institution that does not take its stand on such sacred ground. Perhaps this is what lies behind the anger of many people like Cormac: they seek and expect a place of visibly lived Christianity—of care and compassion, of community and contemplation. Precisely because they are disappointed in these gospel hopes, they sense a greater letdown with the church than with institutions like universities or governments that also fall short of their ideals. The hopes of the Cormacs whom I have known are often grounded in genuinely Christian intuitions.

Although I could recognize and agree with many of his causes of complaint, there remained major differences between my response and his. How could I stay within this flawed church? I had a different sense of things and for two reasons. One was fairly predictable, the other more surprising. The predictable one related to the generation or culture gap between us. Unlike Cormac, who is a child of the seventies, I grew up in a way that gave me stronger roots in Catholicism, through happy experiences of childhood religion, and through inheriting a certain loyalty to the church. Because of the strength of those spiritual memories, I can tolerate the warts of church life because I sense a wider wisdom there. Of course I want the warts removed, or at least reduced, but in practice I don't ever expect an ideal church. I am less shocked than Cormac by the church of sinners that is, alas, our human reality.

Now to the surprising reason: could it be that Cormac remains romantic in his critique because he is too innocent about sin? That is what I found myself saying to him. I knew, of course, that the very word would be strange to him, that he could be allergic to it from childhood. Exactly my point. If his only view of sin came from childhood, then his needle was stuck in this respect. The child's model of wrongdoing as "breaking the rules" would not fit the larger scandals of sin in our world, including the sin of hypocrisy that he discerned within the church.

Innocent About Sin?

This is a large and difficult topic, and I know I am in danger of being misunderstood. It could sound like I'm sidestepping his accusation by changing the agenda: "The church seems corrupt to me." "Ah, but your trouble is that you have no sense of sin." That could come across as a false shifting of the argument. Instead, I intend it as taking his accusation of dishonesty to its ultimate level of seriousness, which in religious language is called sin.

How on earth are we to make sense of sin today, for Cormac, or indeed for anyone who grows out of the obedience model of reality? Already, in thinking about Herod, we have seen something of the powerful forces of deception and evil at work in our world. But the key difference between evil and sin is that sin implies some personal responsibility. To speak of a church of sinners is to acknowledge something that is not at some comfortable distance from us, such as a civil war in a distant land. So what is this thing called sin?

Let me answer with a true story. Several months ago, I was asked to preside at the twelve o'clock Mass in a parish where I had lived for three years. In this area with high levels of unemployment, only a small proportion of people attend church. But those who do attend bring something special and vibrant. Behind the success of the twelve o'clock Mass lies a group of people who meet the previous Monday evening to prepare the liturgy. The priest who is to preside—on this occasion, myself—sits in on this meeting. On this particular Monday in Lent the theme was sin, which at first seemed a gloomy topic. At one point one of the women said, almost in jest, "Could you possibly make sin seem happy? After all, the gospel is meant to be good news." It seemed a tall order, but we took it as our discussion point. I remarked that the Greek word for sin in the gospels comes from archery and actually means "missing the mark." This proved to be the spark that our group imagination needed. One man offered to make a big drawing of a target of circles with an arrow falling short, and this would hang in front of the altar. Another woman suggested that in my homily I should not mention the word sin until the very end, that I should talk about us missing the mark, God's target being lives of love. And so it became the Sunday when *we* (because it was a number of us who collaborated) managed to communicate a deeper sense of sin.

Church: Warts and Wisdom

To return to the central point, and to my response to Cormac, it is as naive to expect the church to show no signs of sin as it would be to expect oneself to be always a paragon of shining goodness, someone who never misses the mark. I fear that such a dismissal of the church remains superficial until it is forced to confront the struggle of good and evil in every human heart. Even though some of the language used about church seems to imply an ideal state of sanctity, that is not the human reality of its members. It is no surprise to find my own flawed humanity mirrored even in the institution that is called to be Christ in this world.

Finally, I want to offer Cormac a double message, even a seemingly contradictory one. You have had too much church, I would say to him, so much so that it has blocked growth in faith in Christ. So forget the church for the moment *if* it helps you enter a deeper journey of religious meaning. But, I would equally insist, in the long run, you will get lost without the church. Without the support of a community and of a tradition, where will you find friends for your road? Life is far too short to waste in lonely questioning. Without some companionship, such as the church at its best can give, you could be condemned to a private search that never finds a language of life with others. It is the isolated fate of many within our Western culture today. So my final answer to Cormac's question would be: I remain within the church for many reasons, but perhaps mainly because I find goodness and strength and even sanctity here. Ultimately I find God. And all this outweighs the sad failures.

It was Jesus himself who told a parable about the Kingdom as a field of wheat where weeds grew as well. When the workers are shocked by the presence of weeds and want to pull them up, the wise owner tells them that to do so would damage the wheat, and that they should wait until the harvest. The parable points to the mixture of good and evil in any human field. Cormac's shock, like that of the workers, was in many ways justified, but a larger vision, like the owner's, would lead to a more compassionate response.

So for me the church is the community that, in spite of human failings, guards the memory of Christ for each new moment of history. Our hearts need reminding of him. Our imaginations need renourishing with him. Our choices need rechallenging by him. Our spirits need renewal in him. And our lives need companionship in following him. The church exists to guide and serve that long adventure of living out the vision that he called the Kingdom. Chesterton once remarked that the church "is the one thing that saves a person from the degrading servitude of being a child of one's own time." And, I would add, from believing one's own little self to be the only measure of meaning.

CHAPTER EIGHT

FALLING TO THEIR KNEES: PRAYER

At the heart of the Magi story is the moment of adoration. It is, we are told, a physical act of reverence that these sages offer to the infant Jesus. It expresses wonder and awe before the presence of God in this child.

Traditionally this moment is celebrated in the feast called Epiphany, and the focus is on the moment of recognition of God in human form. Artists and poets have been fascinated with this scene, often seeing it as a revolution in wisdom. The Magi thought they were bringing gifts to some new human king, but instead found themselves receiving a glimpse of God, with the flow of gifts reversed.

This core moment in the story evokes the many languages of prayer. At the center of every religion is some meeting with God. At the center of Christianity is an encounter with God through Jesus.

How can this meeting happen today? More simply how can we arrive at the threshold of prayer? And what is it like to cross that threshold into some experience of the presence of God?

Agnostics Can Pray

The claim that agnostics can pray has its origin in my contacts with unbelievers. I want to recount one such experience to show that a spiritual life is possible for everyone, independent of religious faith or belonging to a church. It also seems right to approach the question of prayer from "below," as it were, as a human adventure in awareness first of all, even though it is more than that, as we shall see later.

Derek was a politically alert young man. His parents were agnostic and he had been brought up without any religious formation. The school he attended was Catholic and he did quite well in "religious knowledge" without it ever becoming a reality for him. He learned some dogma and some Bible stories. But Derek was artistic in temperament; he was especially gifted in music and liked to express himself in poetry. This was what brought him into personal contact with me for the first time. He wanted to ask my opinion on some poems he had written. They explored his own memories and feelings in a very honest way. Many of them seemed to be about hurts in relationships and about smoldering resentments.

We moved from talking about the texts to talking about the underlying experiences, which centered on his elder brother. Derek had been close to him when they were younger but after his brother's marriage a painful gap seemed to come between them. He was particularly hurt by the fact that whenever they planned some occasion together—an outing, a game of tennis, even a meal at his brother's house—his brother nearly always canceled it at the last moment. This led Derek to wonder whether his sister-in-law disliked him or was not at ease with him, but his own feelings were wounded and confused. At one point in telling me all this, Derek remarked almost flippantly, "If I were a Christian, you could tell me to pray for the grace of forgiveness." "Perhaps you can still pray in your own way, even as an unbeliever," I replied, equally playful and yet serious. "Even without God?" "Why not? Let's call it meditation."

And so it began—our plan to meet together over a few weeks

for guided meditation. The first step was to learn some skills of stillness and to practice them each day. The exercise that seemed to help Derek most was one that is called *vipassana* in the East. This involves letting one's awareness gather round all the various physical sensations of the skin, literally from head to toe. One simply moves the focus of one's awareness, like radar, down all the body surfaces, and back up again. If a person does this several times, slowly and gradually banishing other distractions, it is normal to discover many, varied sensations one is not usually conscious of. The object of the exercise is to provide an anchor of stillness, a rudder for the unruly attention.

Once the self is anchored through this noticing of the senses (and this may easily take ten or fifteen minutes), then the person can listen to the emotions or memories that come from the depths. This is exactly what happened to Derek. He found a place and a time each day to practice this form of focusing for at least ten minutes and then listen to his feelings. I suggested that he get in touch with his feelings of gratitude for just being alive and for his brother in particular. He came back after a few days of this to report that he found it remarkably easy and fruitful. The simple method of creating quiet helped him to relax and he found that his former feelings of anger and resentment were less dominant. He was delighted to be able to recognize more positive emotions within himself and to enjoy them.

Inner Journey Minus God

"But would you call this prayer?" Derek asked me with some doubt in his voice. If prayer means some deliberate reaching out to God, I told him, perhaps it's not prayer, strictly speaking. But put it the other way around. Suppose there is a God. The only God worth believing in would want to reach out to you, and whether or not you recognize that is secondary. When you learn to listen to your deepest self, perhaps you are entering one of the places where God is reaching out to you in shy silence. And that may be the only kind of prayer you are capable of for the moment.

But trust your experience. Don't mind the interpretation of it for now. It is possible that this experience is very human; it is also possible that it is a meeting of your spirit and the Spirit of God. Enjoy the experience and gather the fruits. Explanations can wait.

So Derek, the self-styled atheist or agnostic, continued on his path of meditation. Every few days he came to reflect on his progress, and eventually found himself realizing much more of a sense of wonder and trust within himself than he had been aware of for a long time. "Since when?" I asked. "Probably since child-hood," he replied. Exactly. Derek was getting in touch with the trusting child within him, with that deeper experience of himself that had recently been eclipsed in temporary fashion by the hurts and disappointments caused by his brother. Once he was in touch with this former base of joy and aliveness, with his true self, it was safe to confront the more negative experiences. To have started with them directly would not have helped.

Thus after about ten days of daily quiet times, when Derek was able to relax into the reality of being grateful for his life, I suggested that he continue with the entrance exercise of physical focusing but to go ahead calmly and face his less happy feelings and memories. I gave Derek a scene from the gospel to ponder, from chapter five of Luke. It tells of Jesus borrowing Peter's boat to speak to the crowds. Afterwards, as if to thank him for the use of the boat, Jesus invites Peter to move to deep waters and to let down his nets. Peter responds with a mixture of failure and trust. "We worked hard all night long and caught nothing, but if you say so, I will put out the nets." When he does this, the nets fill to bursting and at the sight of this, Peter, we are told, "fell at the knees of Jesus saying, 'Leave me; I am a sinful man.'" This scene on its own would be rich enough for many a meditation. It is a story of emptiness (nothing all night), of trust (he tries again because Jesus invites him), of fullness and amazement (the huge catch), and then of unworthiness (a sinful man). Derek could easily identify with the first three emotions that echoed his own experiences of failure, of confidence in a friend, and of aliveness or gratitude. But why the sense of unworthiness and why then? Would not a more normal reaction be to thank Jesus or, in more traditional religious language, to "praise the Lord"?

Unworthiness Without Guilt

I have another story, one that stemmed from an extraordinary coincidence. Some years previously, another student had sat in exactly the same chair as Derek and had a similar period of guided prayer—except that in his case it was a prayer rooted in Christian faith. His name was Peter and he ran into a similar puzzle over the reaction of his namesake at this point in the gospel. But as it happened he had a most unusual breakthrough toward a solution. He was celebrating his twenty-first birthday during the university term and, being far from his family, decided to invite a wide circle of student friends to gather in a tavern, at least to begin the night. They all agreed. As the day approached, however, more and more of them begged off, explaining that they couldn't make it that evening. Peter ended up with only four friends, and although disappointed, managed to hide his hurt. They went to the tavern together, but then one of the girls suggested it would be more pleasant to move back to Peter's flat, perhaps buying something to eat on the way. Back they went to a major surprise! On opening the door, he found everyone he had invited and more, and the whole apartment decorated. As he told me later, he collapsed into a chair near the door as they all sang "Happy Birthday" and he felt *unworthy*. At that strange moment he understood the other Peter, and why, when surrounded by giftedness, one realizes one's own poverty. Perhaps it is only when one is "overwhelmed by miracle" (a phrase from William Butler Yeats) that it is safe to face one's shadow side.

All this is a long way of saying that for Derek to deal with his churned up resentments and other negative reactions, it was necessary first to ground himself in gratitude and in a sense of the goodness of life. And he could do all this at some depth of self-listening without explicit faith. He had the courage to face those "deep waters," and I had confidence that if he remained faithful to letting his net down daily into those waters, he would not be far from the Kingdom. Even though no huge conversions of faith occurred for Derek, he certainly discovered a spiritual wavelength within himself and arrived at new freedoms that he needed—as we shall see.

Armed with the gospel text as an anchor for his imagination, Derek was now ready to deal with his own anger, guilt, and hurt. As before, he was to create inner peace (the physical awareness exercise), next gather his sense of gratitude from the previous week (like the full net), and only then pause deliberately on his more painful emotions, seeking to hear them and say goodbye to what might be unworthy in them. Approached in this spirit, the negatives could be purified of what might be unworthy of Derek himself (shallow or prejudiced reactions) or of others (being too quick to judge them harshly).

His second week of meditation proved more difficult in some ways, but ultimately it was fruitful as well. The difficulties arose from a certain resistance to the zones of pain, and as Derek discovered, from a fear that he would find himself exposed as equally to blame. But even though the efforts of some days seemed to lead nowhere, he kept going, until on one particular day during the silence he discovered himself in tears. He had been thinking about his brother and about the gap that had opened up between them. Suddenly he was overwhelmed by a sense of sadness, as if his brother had died, and he realized that much of his resentment was in fact a kind of mourning over the loss of his brother in marriage. He had come in touch with his own vulnerability and loneliness, and it was easy enough now to forgive his brother and even, as was equally necessary, to forgive himself.

From Healing to Choice

When we met to reflect on the week, Derek had arrived at a clearer view of the pain that he had broached in our first conversation. He was able to own his responsibility in clinging to his angers. A certain honesty had opened a door to new freedom for him. He could now handle his relationship with his brother more serenely. Thus in a sense we had finished what we set out to do. Or had we? I asked Derek if he thought there were more areas to visit through this kind of daily meditation. Without any hesitation he replied, "Yes, what am I to do with my life and why?"

It was as if clearing up the negatives were not enough. Now that they had been addressed, now that he was discovering a daily avenue into his own depths, the compass of his desire swung in a fresh direction—toward decision and commitment, with an accompanying hunger for self-meaning. He explained to me that he was left with a new but happy dissatisfaction with himself. All the explorings of these weeks had put him in touch with an inner self that he had previously ignored. He looked back on the way he had been living as a kind of helpless drifting, happy enough in its own way but missing out on many possibilities. So at one point he asked, "Where do you think I am in all of this?" I found myself saying, "You've found the child in you; now you want to find the adult." It was a little too neat a summary, yet it had its truth. Up to now his inner journey had enabled Derek to enter the realm of feelings of trust and wonder, and later of vulnerability and pain. Now that he was able to embrace this child dimension of himself with both courage and compassion, it was only natural to want to focus on owning his adult future. Healing of any kind usually opens the door to hope.

For the next week we agreed on a different strategy. Derek would continue to use whatever skills of stillness helped him to find a steady level of listening. But then he would focus on people whom he admired in any way, harvesting the memories of goodness that he had glimpsed in others. It could involve famous spiritual leaders such as Mohandas Gandhi or Martin Luther King, Jr., or people in his own circle, like his mother who had come through a major illness with her usual serenity and humor. After letting his imagination rest on whatever moved him in contemplating such heroic figures, Derek was then to reflect and see what this called forth in his own humanity. My hope and aim in suggesting this was that he would awaken and identify some of the desires of his heart, and so find an answer to his own question.

It proved fruitful well beyond what I had expected. Derek returned the following week with a different energy in his voice. "It's very simple," he said; "I want to lead a generous life from now on." He went on to describe how he found himself drawn in fantasy to hold a long conversation with, of all people, Jesus. He had tried out some other ideal people but gradually discovered that his image of Jesus, even though vague in many ways, was a more powerful attraction for dialogue. Somewhere in his past he had encountered the saying "Love one another as I have loved you" and this formed the hinge of their imaginary conversation. "Don't get me wrong," Derek warned me; "I'm as agnostic as before about all the God stuff. Just because I was imagining Jesus doesn't mean I was praying as you might do. But it did seem to release my hopes and I know that I want to make a difference in this world as he did. That's something I think I can hang on to, even though I don't know what form it could take in practice."

Listening to this surprising development, I felt a great reverence for the point at which Derek had now arrived. Part of me would have loved to steer him toward a more explicit Christian faith but another, wiser part of me felt that the journey into freedom he had experienced would surely bear fruit in the long term, and perhaps in the direction of faith. He was certainly more open than ever before, both to his own human call and to the depths discovered through his inner adventure. I decided to trust in the rhythm of the Spirit who had been at work (at least as I saw it) during these weeks. To have made an option for a generous life, one that was inspired by the figure of Jesus, was sufficient fruit for the moment.

The Suppressed Spiritual

Having decided to leave behind these fairly intense exercises in meditation, Derek and I found ourselves reflecting back on the whole experience. "Do you think you have changed much?" I

asked him. "Yes and no," he replied. "In one way, I'm delighted
with my discovery of a process of listening to reality. That's a major change. I never knew such a wavelength was possible for me.
But the change I needed was not what I first thought. It wasn't
simply a matter of sorting out my confused feelings about my
brother. It was much more; I needed a rudder for my own existence as a whole. And you were able to provide one from the religious tradition. I imagine you would describe the entire thing in
more spiritual language, would you?"

Yes, the inspiration behind my suggestions had come from the
Spiritual Exercises of Ignatius of Loyola. From that famous text,
and from my own repeated experience of its process, I had the
conviction that graces (or, in everyday language, freedoms) usually come in a certain sequence. Thus I advised Derek not to face his
more negative feelings until he had spent time getting in touch
with a sense of wonder and gratitude. Later, when he had worked
through the woundedness a bit, it was natural for him to lay out
his agenda of searching into options and choices.

The three stages that he had experienced could be named as basic trust, followed by what the old spiritual tradition would term
the purgative and illuminative ways, or in more contemporary
language: get in touch, face the shadow, own your life. The sad
thing is that in today's noisy culture many people are seduced
into scatteredness and never experience their full potential. What
was special about Derek's spiritual exercises is that his agnosti-
cism proved no barrier to his traveling on a road of spiritual liberation influenced by the Christian tradition.

Finally, it is worth recording his own conclusions when he
looked back later on his unusual journey. "If this is spirituality,"
he remarked, "why is it such a closely guarded secret? Why is religion, as most people find it, so associated with boring rituals
and empty words? Even if I can't make sense of God, at least I can
glimpse the depths where God might be waiting to be found. But
most believers are deprived of this level of self-discovery. To me
it seems as if religion is failing its own core vision."

In his own way Derek was voicing a major critique of religion in practice, one that sounds with a special urgency today. To return to the images of the Magi story, where can people find a genuine "house" experience today, where adoration is possible in a transformative and creative way? The hunger for the contemplative dimension of religion has never been more acute than in this era of sensate stimulation. This leads us to another example of a different explorer in that direction.

From Literature to Silence

It was after an evening class on George Eliot's *Middlemarch* that I first talked to Joanne. She approached me as I was going to my office, and surprised me by saying, "Thank you for a most spiritual lecture." "That's an unusual compliment," I replied. We ended up talking for an hour or so. By "spiritual" she meant that the session had touched on some crucial issues: how to live without the old clarities about God, how to cope with the spiritual loneliness of any searcher nowadays, how to salvage some religiousness when formal religion fails to touch lives, how to find food for the transition from egoism to sympathy, and how a woman can make any difference in the real world, or must she live an "unhistoric" life? (The word in quotes is George Eliot's.)

So we spoke about literature as a long dialogue about basics. Many imaginative writers, whether believers or not, have been engaged in a search for ultimates and have formed, as it were, a conspiracy of spirituality. They have promoted suspicion about the complacencies of their cultures. At the same time, and with a certain shyness, they have defended non-rationalist intuitions of truth. Not only was there George Eliot's quest for a substitute wisdom, an ethics of compassion in the seeming absence of God. Think of how D.H. Lawrence passionately defends the God-flame within humanity. Then there is Aldous Huxley's conversion in mid-career from cynical satirist to explorer in search for mystical awareness. Or T.S. Eliot's similar emergence from a despairing poetry of fragments into one that seeks to evoke religious experience across the boundaries of religions. Or more recently, Saul Bellow's satire of the stifled soul in crowded cities, as he leads his central figures to liberation, to trusting their hearts' hunches, where "the depths of the spirit are never overcrowded." Or Patrick White, who seeks to awaken a sense of mystery and "to give professed unbelievers glimpses of their own unprofessed religious factor." Or Flannery O'Connor's assaults on the armor-plated pride of modernity, humbling her central figures into knowing their need for revelation. What about William Butler Yeats, or E.M. Forster? Or even Samuel Beckett, whose work centers on our comic inability to accept meaninglessness and who is obsessed with a religious-like hunger that will not die? And the list could go on.

In that first conversation with Joanne, as we explored this vast field of literature, I found myself reaching for a quotation from T.S. Eliot. What he once remarked about Nathaniel Hawthorne and Henry James could easily apply to this whole tradition of imagination in quest of meaning, that they displayed "indifference to religious dogma and at the same time exceptional awareness of spiritual reality." At this point, Joanne turned the focus on me, asking if this latent spirituality was a justification for a priest to teach literature in a secular university. "It was part of it," I replied, saying that I enjoyed the challenge of being where worlds converge. But what about revelation and contemplation? They were certainly the foundations of any religion, countered Joanne. Were they not in effect banished by the secular ethos, and was that not a frustration for me? Yes, indeed, teaching theology is forbidden in the university founded by Cardinal Newman, which must leave him spinning in his grave. And yes, in practice it is "not on" for me to speak of explicitly religious horizons, such as Scripture and prayer. Except in private, when invited, as with Joanne now.

How Do You Pray?
At first I had imagined her to be some variety of agnostic, perhaps a contemporary echo of George Eliot. How wrong I was! It gradu-

ally emerged that she had a profound commitment to an inner life, that she had explored Buddhism and the spiritual side of Jung, and that she gave some regular time to daily meditation. What she was not sure of was her relationship to the Catholicism and Christianity of her upbringing. She had not rejected it, but neither was it in the forefront of her spiritual life at present. Her key question to me, when she managed to voice it, proved to be a curious one. How did I, as a Christian, pray, and above all, did I trust the silence? Behind Joanne's inquiry, as it turned out, was a sense that Christianity seemed less contemplative than Eastern religions, that what most people found in Catholicism were rituals, rules, and prayers (plural—like Our Fathers and Hail Marys), and therefore that silent meditation, such as she had discovered and developed, seemed discouraged or at least neglected.

Alas, what Joanne voiced is a common impression that is both true and false. It is true that many people never get the opportunity to acquaint themselves with the spiritual tradition of the West. But it is false that Catholicism lacks ways of contemplative wisdom. An encounter with mystery lies at the heart of Christianity. The definiteness of Christ as Incarnate God and the concreteness of his new command of love should in no way diminish the mystical core of Christian faith. All too often the pressures of the practical have relegated the spiritual to an optional extra, making it seem a specialization for religious rather than the birthright of every believer, or allowing it to be taken up by the world of art and literature with a richness frequently absent in official religion.

What could I say to Joanne about prayer? Her question was not about the theology of prayer but about my own experience of what she called "silence." In this sense she was putting me on the spot and looking for a personal answer. At the time, and in several subsequent meetings, I tried to meet her question, as well as to hear her own side of things. What I want to communicate here is something of what we discovered together, through our mutual efforts to dialogue about silence and the spirit.

Defeating the Monkeys

I admitted to Joanne that I am unsteadily faithful to a daily space of silence that I call prayer. I say "unsteadily" because prayer has often been sold short or performed without care, or just jettisoned under pressure. But usually it is there somehow and it is something very important to me. Without prayer I fear I would be even more stuck with a "heart of stone" and less in touch with the "heart of flesh" (Ezekiel 36:26). Over the years it has been a slowly changing adventure that is hard to put into words, but it has certainly moved from something more complex to something more simple. When I think back now on the complicated "points" I used to make as a novice—heady ideas on the Scriptures, written at night for the morning's meditation—I feel a thousand miles from that older self. Gradually I grew to prefer silence and to think of it as the language of God. Not that it is always easy to rest in total quiet. (The tree of self is full of jumpy monkeys, as a guru once said to me in India.) Where Joanne and I found much common ground was in the area of skills for stillness, and how we need ways of centering the scattered self (somewhat as described in talking about Derek). I surprised Joanne by saying that I have no difficulty in praying, but hastened to add that I have huge difficulty in getting myself to the threshold of prayer. Perhaps the secret lies in self-patience when the monkeys are jumpy, and in having ways to tranquilize them. The problem is having the courage to create the stillness, but once that point is passed, prayer happens naturally.

In this respect, and on a practical level. I shared one piece of advice with Joanne. If those first few minutes are crucial as setting an inner atmosphere either of listening or of unease, then are there any practical helps that can steer that opening time? I think there are, and I call my formula *roca* (the Spanish word for rock). Each letter stands for something that facilitates the possibility of deeper prayer.

R stands for reverence, a fundamental requirement; if I remember who I am reaching out to, then both physically and internally

I will have an attitude of reverence. The story of the Magi, in fact, mentions both the outer and inner: falling down and adoring.

O stands for offering, in the sense of promising the time and the effort to keep one's appointment, to be present from the heart.

C stands for centering, for all that range of methods that can quiet the frivolous monkeys within. It is possible to take one's temperature very quickly, so to speak, and to know whether the conditions of silence are present or not. If quiet comes naturally, then forget about techniques of centering, but if it is one of those distracted days, then time is well spent in laying the foundations for listening. Usually this means having the humility to let *one* sense impression gather the straying mind: repeating a phrase, listening to sounds, becoming aware of the touch of one's hands, looking at the flame of a candle, even voicing one's feelings aloud if circumstances allow. These or other techniques can, if patiently attended to, work wonders for stillness.

Finally, *A* stands for asking, and here is where Joanne found herself resisting the simplicity of my suggestions. She could follow me up to this point but to stress asking seemed to her like the "old-fashioned" prayer of petition. Is it ever old-fashioned? I asked. Is it not rather at the heart of prayer to come before God in need? Asking gives focus to desire, and prayer is the language of desire. Ask for what? For the big things, like peace, love, wisdom, and the Spirit.

Awareness or Relationship?

Our disagreement over prayer of petition pointed to a more basic difference. Joanne was not sure that she was praying to a personal God. For her, it was easier to look on meditation time as an awareness exercise, rather than to think of herself as entering into any relationship with a God beyond her. For me, the awareness exercise was only a means, an essential means, to the contact with God which was the aim of prayer. This was a significant difference of emphasis and of interpretation (and one to which we would return), but the ground of our dialogue remained. In

Joanne's own words, it lay in the spiritual experience of silence.

With respect for her hesitations, I first want to evoke this experience in words that do not stress the relationship with God; later, we can bring in the explicitly Christian sense of prayer. To immerse oneself in silence has become a luxury within the rhythms of life today. To many people it seems strange to set time aside for total quiet; to me it seems strange not to. It is within such quiet space that the heart tunes into a wavelength that is otherwise unreachable. It dares to exit from everyday concerns and to be rescued from the blinders of the practical. It enters into the un-understandable. What seems like withdrawal opens out into deeper involvement with everything and everyone. From the horizon of silence, the heart can see through the small comforts and small concerns, the shoddy stuff that kidnaps us (Herod's plot again); but nourished on silence the heart can expand into a compassion that both consoles and makes demands.

This kind of silence is a healing and strengthening space, a place where the daily dishonest gap between words and deeds is bridged. It is hard to describe what happens there except that the self moves from emptiness and the shame of its shadows into belonging. It moves from unworthy, fragile peace into costly and genuine peace. This time of listening adjusts the heart's uncertain compass toward love. Without that acid test of giving and compassion, the whole thing could be concerned only with self. Learning to love is the only worthy goal for all this silence. Indeed there is nothing special about silence—except that, as life goes on, it is often the best language of listening and learning. In the exposure to silence there is little room for dishonest games. Besides, it is our safest language for mystery and for God, well beyond the inadequacies of mere words.

Specifics of Christianity
Something of all that and more must have happened to the Magi in their moment of adoration. Indeed, the famous scene offers a perfect example of where Joanne could meet the contemplative

note of Christianity: it unites the silent encounter with mystery, central to all religions, with the more personal presence of God in Jesus, specific to Christianity. All the great religions of the East focus on searching for the divine, and are marvelously rich in stressing silence. But Christianity has a different starting point and makes a more startling claim. It is not so much that we have to search for God (that is true but secondary), as that God has searched for us "at many moments in the past and by many means" (the opening of the Letter to the Hebrews). This ultimately includes Jesus, who has been sent to find us and to show us the way.

What might Joanne find or imagine in that Magi moment of adoration? Those wise travelers had come to bring gifts to a new king. Did they penetrate the identity of this particular king? The gospel does not say, but it lets us suppose that they did, even with some obscure faith without words. If so, they experienced a reversal, a change in the direction of their journey. They thought they were the gift-bringers, but they now discover themselves to be the receivers of a much greater gift. In that prayer of adoration, their hearts must have realized something of the revolution and revelation present before them.

At the core of Christianity is a God who comes to us in our humanity. This reaching out by God is so simple and yet so radically different from anything found in Eastern religions. It lifts our burden of lonely spiritual journeying. It promises a side-by-side companionship on the road from life into Life. Thus the center of our silence is inhabited. It is no longer an absence but a presence, moreover a presence with a human face. Such a conversion from an abstract belief in God to a more personal faith in Jesus is what should define a Christian, and yet it can be sadly rare even among church-goers.

A Christ-discovery of this kind changed the tone of Joanne's silence. Slowly and over months she continued her daily spiritual space, but now she turned more to the Scriptures for nourishment. She kept her practice of quiet, but it now became a wordless encounter with a friend, a conversation of the heart beyond language. Sometimes, of course, she would use words, would ponder gospel scenes, but the key to her prayer was a resting in a new silence of presence.

One day Joanne came to tell me of another discovery, one she made herself with the help of some reading. "Why," she asked, "did you not tell me about the Trinity?" "I presumed you knew, and besides, it seemed too complicated to go into." But the opposite was true; the reality of Father, Son, and Spirit had become for Joanne a rich anchor for her prayer and her life. Previously, of course, she had known about the Trinity, in the sense of having heard the doctrine. But she had never known its relevance for her. What she had now discovered, however, was that the three persons answered to three dimensions of her life.

The Trinity as Real

The Father is the God beyond us whom "no one has ever seen" (John 1:18), and hence for Joanne the God of mystery, encountered in a prayer of silence. The Son, by contrast, showed us God as one like ourselves, one who struggled and loved, who said that as often as we "did this to the least of these," we did it to him. For Joanne this other face of God is encountered mainly in the call of others and in serving the hungers of our wounded world, as well as encountered in the Scriptures, the sacraments, and prayer that speaks directly to Christ. The Spirit of God within our hearts, leading us toward love, helping us to recognize our gifts (1 Corinthians 2:12) and to set them free for others. This is the real presence of God within every person, believer or unbeliever; and this Spirit "expresses our longings" in a way that could never be put into words (Romans 8:26).

Joanne had discovered her own sense of the Trinity and her own answer to the question, Where is your God? God is in silence mystery: Father. God continues in all humanity: Son. God dwells in every heart and conscience: Spirit. This gave her an exciting new synthesis for prayer and faith. Gradually she moved from being committed to the vaguely spiritual to being committed to the Christian vision of the spiritual—and she lost nothing on the way. What had started as an interest in interiority had broadened out to become genuine prayer. What had begun as awareness exercises in stillness became both personal and interpersonal. At the outset Joanne's focus was on the adventure of the inner self; now she found herself drawn into finding her place within the bigger drama of this struggling world.

A footnote to this story of Joanne: I have never known an atheist who fully appreciated the Trinity. Perhaps the god that atheists refuse is the "lonely God in the sky" as often as not, and they simply do not know the Trinity except as a piece of distant mumbo jumbo. Yet, as Walter Kasper has argued, the "grammar" of perfect love is summed up in the community of Father, Son, and Spirit, and is *the* Christian answer to the God-question. When Joanne began to pray with a sense of Trinity, she was arriving at what is specifically Christian. In my experience, this appreciation is not beyond our grasp, nor for theologians only. It is something quite simple. The gospels more than once tell of Jesus being led by the Spirit and of his praying to the Father on the mountain. As Joanne discovered for herself, when we pray, we enter into and echo that encounter. We are invited to turn *toward* the Father, *with* Jesus, and so to pray *in* the Spirit. We have then a rich and threefold answer to the question, Where is your God? God is *beyond* us; God is *beside* us; God is *within* us. Or to come back again to our Magi metaphors, God is in the silent adoration, and in the giving, and in the dream.

CHAPTER NINE

CHOOSING TO GIVE

The moment of the Magi story most frequently shown in art is the presentation of the gifts. It is usually depicted as an exotic scene in keeping with the rich gifts mentioned by Matthew.

Once again we can approach the episode as capturing an essential strand in Christian living: we are here to give of what we have been given.

Where do we learn generosity of heart? What forms does it take in different circumstances? Perhaps the transparent generosity of the saints has always helped to make sense of faith. Even our confused culture is moved when it glimpses God through the extraordinary goodness of ordinary people.

Pedro Pablo

Many of the stories told about people in these pages use changed names, and some disguise the identities still further in order to avoid embarrassing the real people in question. On this occasion, however, I use no such disguise. It is most unlikely that the young boy concerned will ever see these pages. He is living in a poor barrio in Venezuela, but if by chance this book were to be translated into Spanish, I would be delighted for him to read about himself. He might even have forgotten the incident. I will never forget it. It was something that summed up—in one eloquent but simple act—the spirit of giving found in the gospels.

It happened like this. In 1987 I was spending some time in San Felix, a city in east Venezuela. I was staying with a Jesuit community living in the middle of a large barrio with some 40,000 people in one parish. Conditions were basic. Some were living in huts and others had developed their huts over the years into what might be called brick cottages. At the time of my visit, there was a shortage of tap water, in spite of the fact that we were beside the huge Orinoco river. The contrast of two worlds never hit me more than one morning when I wanted to wash. The only tap water available was an inch or so scooped from our communal barrel, and this had a few dead flies in it. As it happened, my bit of soap had "Japan Air Lines" on it. The comedy of it seemed to point to the tragedy of our divided planet. I could remember sipping *sake* in that luxurious plane; here I was washing in an inch of dirty water.

Across from our community lived a very poor family with many children. There were two mothers and about twelve children under one roof. I never saw the fathers; they were away looking for work in another part of the country. One of the children, a boy of about eleven called Pedro Pablo, used to come across to our place fairly often, sometimes to see if any spare mangos had fallen from our tree during the night. (They used to thud on the tin roof and wake me up!)

He became friendly with me. For him I was something of a novelty, so white and unable to speak Spanish properly. We arranged to exchange lessons because he was beginning to learn English at school. This particular day the children were all sent home from school after an hour or two, because, without water, they had no toilet facilities. So Pedro Pablo came over to me as my teacher and pupil. We were swapping simple words like "hand" and "tree" when I noticed that he was continually rubbing his stomach under his shirt. I asked him, *"Tienes hambre?"* "Are you hungry?" He nodded a bit shyly. When had he last eaten? Yesterday morning. Was there nothing in his house? Nobody had anything to eat except a few mangos. I asked him if he would like a big sandwich. Again he nodded, a bit embarrassed. Although we had not much in our kitchen, we had the makings of a sandwich. But when I made it and gave it to him, he didn't eat it. "Aren't you going to eat it?" I can still remember his reply in Spanish and I think the words will stay with me for a long time. *"Voy a llevar a mi mamá que está embarazada."* "I'll bring it to my mother who is pregnant." And off he went, leaving me stunned. I sat there for a long time in silence.

Comment seems superfluous. I sensed that I had glimpsed Christ's spirit alive in a poor child. It was one of those profoundly moving moments when one feels in touch with the heart of life, with the reason for being here at all. It is good to add that the story did not end there. Pedro Pablo's generosity was contagious, and I found myself able to arrange that, at least for those days, there would be no more hunger in that household. That may have been a happy ending in the small scale of one family and in the short term of a few weeks. But what of the larger cry of the majority of this hungry world? That needs a more imaginative giving, a more uphill effort to change. And that too is the call of the Kingdom now.

In this respect, I think of that final and most radical of the Kingdom parables of Jesus, the picture of the last judgment. It makes no mention of God, but only of loving deeds or their absence, and it ends with a revolutionary identification of Jesus with all the wounded of history. "In so far as you did this to one of the least of mine, you did it to me" (Matthew 25:40). I recall seeing a cartoon of this once, which in its own way captured a key aspect of the parable for our time. There was a large courthouse with "Last Judgment" on the dome, and with many doors marked for various categories of sinners: robbers, adulterers, embezzelers, and so on. Over one door was written "unbelievers" and out of this door a stream of people came jumping with delight. The caption read, "Faith isn't on the exam paper."

Ours is an unbelieving age. For all sorts of cultural reasons, there is a crisis in the language of faith, more than in faith as such. Many people find themselves victims of uncertainty over many things, faith included. This would apply to most of the students I have known in recent years. Even when they held on to some of their inherited religion, they often remained unsure in matters of faith. Yet, again and again, I found them wanting to give of themselves in some way. It is as if faith is a chord with several notes, and the note that rings strongest within today's culture is the note of offering one's gifts. That moment in the Magi story sparks a secret generosity within many a young person, even when he or she cannot make sense of some explanations of faith. If these generous desires remain latent or even secret, it is often because they have not been recognized or called forth into action. In terms of the Magi imagery, it is as if nobody comes with the key to their coffers. "Opening their treasures, they offered him gifts."

Another Teenager
Several years ago, I became acquainted with a family of Irish origin but long settled in the U.S. Among the children was one who was looked on as wild and troublesome. He was sixteen. Let us call him Sean. A crisis arose in the family. He was diagnosed as suffering from venereal disease. As an outsider and a priest, and as somebody he related to a little, I was asked to speak to him. Not the easiest prospect but to my surprise Sean took the initiative and asked me to come to his room. Once there, our dialogue went in an unexpected direction. He produced a poem that he

wanted me to read, and which he later gave me as a present. Part of it went as follows:

> They think I'm just a piece of dirt
> as my father said to me;
> it seems that I don't care a damn
> for anyone but me.
> But they don't know the hopes I have
> locked up inside of me,
> they never asked about the poem
> I'd like my life to be.
> If they ever saw this, they'd sneer and mock
> 'cos the me they choose to see
> is the cause of this whole family shame—
> true, but only part of me.
> But what I want, after all this mess,
> is that some day they'll see
> that I do care and seek my space
> to live and give and *be*.
> I want a different sort of life,
> not one of simply me,
> not grabbing but giving of myself
> Christ-like and tenderly.

This is a real cry from the heart. It expresses a longing for recognition of his generosity, something deeper than all the hurt and guilt. That secret self can remain under lonely lock and key until somebody offers a word of recognition, as I was able to do. Indeed, later that evening I managed to have Sean show some of his poems to his father and mother. It was a healing moment when he read one of them aloud, and I could see a strange pride in his parents' eyes. Their Sean was something other than a shame and a troublemaker.

This may seem romantic and soft. Perhaps. I am simply witnessing to my constant experience that behind bad news, good

news often lurks. Behind the rapist, the murderer, the addict—
and I have met them all—a basic generosity waits in secret and
has never been quenched. One could put all this in more exalted
language and speak of fundamental options that people live by. Is
anyone wholly evil? I doubt it. Everyone falls into shames and
guilts of various kinds. Some cause terrible pain to others. But the
flow of each life is a tussle of options, between grabbing or giving,
as Sean's poem put it. Or, as he also said, between not caring a
damn, and struggling to live "Christ-like and tenderly."

Perhaps this is the image of Christ that speaks to our present
culture—the sense of someone living completely for others, a life
totally given. Many people, like Sean, may remain blocked or distant from the fullness of faith—from church, prayer, or any real
understanding of the gospel. But they are seldom without this
hunch of the heart that the greatest goodness shone in Jesus, and
that somehow they, too, want to live that way.

What happens to this desire in practice? There can be a painful
gap between generosity hoped for and generosity lived. Pre-
Christian philosophers, like Plato, recognized that nobody actually chooses evil, but that anybody can be deceived into choosing
false good. This is where, in our story, Herod and his agents are at
work, seeking to limit those hopes of Sean or of anyone else to the
level of mere desire. Fruitless wishes do no damage to Herod's
system. Christians, however, are realists about the struggles en-
tailed in living out the goodness in each person. That is where
they see two crucial forces enter the human fray: the church and
the Spirit. We have already seen how isolation weakens resolve
and how community is vital to stay on the wise way.

Christians also believe that the Spirit is at work in all hearts,
like a slow sculptor shaping beauty from granite. This will be the
focus of our next section, the Magi's "dream."

CHAPTER TEN

THE DREAM AND THE SPIRIT

There is no indication in the Magi story that they would have not returned to Herod with the news about Bethlehem were it not for the dream. Humanly they had been deceived by him, so much so that it took a direct message from God to alert them to the falsehood. About this we are told only that they were "warned in a dream" not to return to the king. We do not know the content of the dream.

In the Bible, dreams are frequently the way in which God speaks to people from within. The dream of the Magi was how they were guided by the Spirit and protected from dangers.

Can this happen today? Does revelation continue? Where do people find wisdom to see through the sham? How are we guided now in the key decisions on our journey?

The Language of Commitment

In his book *Stages of Faith*, James Fowler makes a crucial distinction between the faith capacities of a teenager and those of a young adult. The teenager lives an adventure of relationships and in this way establishes his or her sense of identity. So the faith language characteristic of the late teens involves an interpersonal awareness of God. Even though it may remain shy and inarticulate, Christ is imaged as some kind of friend. But when one enters the twenties, another potential emerges: a faith based more on decision and lived out as a commitment, even against a tide of social pressures. Where the teenager will follow the crowd, or need to find support within a community of peers, the young adult is better able to stand independently. Where previously the typical pattern was one of changing relationships, at this time the possibility of marriage becomes real. The young adult is also prepared for a faith rooted in choice rather than relying on the solidarity of some group. If Fowler's insights hold good, as I believe they do, it means that there is an invitation in our humanity to expand our language of faith as life progresses. In this way faith, though rooted in God, becomes a long adventure of human change.

I have noticed something of this transition from adolescence to adulthood many times during my years of university work. The personal issues raised by the younger students, especially those in their first year, were often connected with relationships or friendships. Typical concerns were with parents or loneliness or self-image or intimacy. But by the time students arrived at their third year, things had often changed. Their focus now became some variant on "What am I going to do?" or "How do you go about making a decision?" The shift of agenda may be due in part to the looming reality of life-beyond-study, but it is also connected with that transition in human development, which Fowler highlights, from a phase of relating and belonging to being able to decide and commit oneself in a new way. Theologian Bernard Lonergan stresses that this is a crisis point in a person's freedom, when she or he finds out that it is up to oneself to decide what to make of that self: "Freedom decides what freedom is to be. The opposite is drifting."

Since there is much less support for faith in today's culture than there was a generation ago, this capacity for commitment has also become a vital area for religious formation. It is crucial to help people first to awaken to the need for faith-as-decision and then to have the steadiness to carry that decision through into life. In terms of our Magi model, it is not only a matter of trusting the light and surviving the darkness, but of seeing through Herod's pressures and resisting them. Then and only then can good decisions be made.

In the Magi's case this level of wisdom came through a dream, which can symbolize the deep self where God speaks to people from within. It is an image of how God "even at night directs my heart" (Psalm 16:7). Just as the star offers a positive invitation to search, the dream serves a more negative role of discerning the deceptions. Even in everyday speech, we say about some problem that it is good to "sleep on it," and often enough we wake up clearer on an issue than when we went to bed.

It seems that the Magi visited their inner world in sleep and that in those strange depths the Spirit was able to show the "world" of Herod to be wrong. But perhaps the dream level has further significance for faith. It is a zone of self-communication beyond the limitations of everyday consciousness. It is beyond language; instead, it exploits the richness of the imagination. It is beyond the practicality of the left side of the brain; instead, it liberates the logic of intuition. It is beyond the externality of the waking self; instead, its wisdom comes from another wavelength. And in this biblical example, it seems also to be beyond a merely human wisdom. Instead, it is a space of revelation where they are guided to "the complete truth" (John 16:13), or to adapt the words of St. Paul, it is an instance of how "the Spirit joins self with our spirit" (Romans 8:13).

Struggles of Choice
How can we make decisions rooted in faith? How do we get in

touch with the level symbolized by the dream? How in practice do we experience the guidance of the Spirit? Here are two contrasting examples to illustrate this process of decision making in a horizon of faith. The story of Tony will flesh out the actual process of making a major choice, while that of Karen shows what may be needed before the time is ripe for any decision making.

Even from mid-teens, Karen was a conscientious searcher for spiritual values to live by. Brought up in a fairly religious family, she conformed to her parents' expectations of church practice, even through periods of unease and distaste. She always believed in God, but this God was a somewhat stern judge who induced guilt and remained distant. Luckily, with the help of a good retreat experience she managed to overcome some of these blocks and to ground her faith in a sense of Christ. This came about for Karen through learning to pray the gospels more personally. In this way she emerged from her childhood models and during her late teens found a more nourishing basis for faith. So far her story was a classic one of moving beyond a merely inherited belonging or conformity into an interpersonal language of faith.

My contact with Karen came at a later stage when, at twenty-one, she was beginning to wonder about choices and even about the possibility of a special vocation. It seemed a genuine question in tune with her prior experience, but whenever she tried to think it through, she kept coming back to me with litanies of self-complaint. She was getting nowhere. She didn't seem able to do anything steadily; she seldom prayed any more, and gradually dropped any regular church-going. Nevertheless, there was a strong faith there, and a high idealism, awakened by the pain of others, about serving Christ.

Karen often spoke of being moved by people on the margins of society, the dropouts, people with AIDS, addicts. But what she called her "unsteadiness" continued and she felt blocked from making any decision. She experienced no lasting peace, which usually accompanies a good decision. For my part, I did not know what might be troubling Karen or defeating her hopes. Then one day a light dawned for both of us. I was summarizing some of my impressions of her generosity, and at one point asked her how she felt about it. Karen's response was immediate, if a bit embarrassed. "I don't think I was listening, really. I can't take praise. I just turn off and go back to being preoccupied."

It was a most revealing moment and indeed a turning point. From pausing on that honest answer, we discovered at least two enemies to the climate needed for a decision. The first was that she thought of herself as a fraud, never able to satisfy the perfection expected of her. Expected by whom? By parents and by a parental kind of God. (This of course is a paraphrase of a longer conversation.) And the second source of unreadiness came from the fact that she had hardly any close friendships and none at all with men. In short, Karen was handicapped through an excessive perfectism and a lack of intimacy with peers. We had been pushing against the wrong door.

Before she could come to the threshold of a good decision, and especially one that might involve a life choice, Karen needed to work on those two areas. Dismantling the oppressive and parental voices (internalized voices, not necessarily her real parents) was something that she could talk through with me or with anyone she found helpful. My hunch was that once this liberation from self-negatives was underway, the second area would take care of itself in time, and with a little courage, she could risk reaching out.

And so it has been. Karen's journey toward new confidence has gone through a few years of slow and undramatic expansion. She has stopped being crippled by the judging ghosts, as she calls them, even though they can still haunt her in small ways. She is gradually finding herself open to deep friendship. Her story remains incomplete as I write. It is a story of quiet struggle and honesty. It is a story of generosity that had to pause and grow before finding its true language.

This summary of one person's search highlights the uniqueness of each life as a mixture of fragility and strength. As with Karen, decisions are seldom made smoothly. They may require that we first tackle various "unfreedoms." But a good decision is worth whatever struggle is involved.

The Stained Glass Experience

Tony's situation was different. It was a question of a marriage choice and more particularly of a certain confusion of feelings at the prospect of announcing his and Helen's engagement. There was no doubt in Tony's mind that their relationship was the best he had ever known, that a marvelous companionship had grown between them. But was this love? Did they really share the same values? Could they risk the commitment of marriage? These and other questions began to plague him as the time of decision approached. It had already been agreed privately between them, but going public was a more fearful step, at least for Tony. Suddenly small things gave rise to conflict, such as how they would tell their parents, or whether or not to have an engagement party. Tony came to talk things over with me and after a while it seemed to both of us that although he was probably just suffering from nerves, it would be worthwhile to listen to the message of his feelings.

Since Tony was a firm believer, my suggestion was that he approach his decision making in a prayerful spirit, looking on the marriage choice as a vocation. I offered him my own brief definition of a vocation as a "willingness that stays happy." It may be short, but each word counts. A vocation needs the three ingredients: a willingness to give one's life in this way, a capacity to stand the test of time, and, if authentic, peace and joy will result. One might object that my definition makes no explicit mention of faith. I take that for granted and presume that the Spirit most often works and speaks through our humanity.

More concretely, I proposed a "stained glass window" exercise to Tony. He was to imagine himself in a room with two stained glass windows. One of them depicts his own future married to Helen. The other shows him married to another woman or living in some other way. First of all, he was to spend time praying for openness, realizing that God is active in his life, and asking to know and respond to whatever might be best. Next I asked him to give at least half an hour, separately, to entering into each alternative. Indeed, he was to do the two parts of this exercise on different days, thus letting his mind rest on the issues even outside the exercise proper.

So on the first day Tony was to enter into a fantasy of being married to Helen, and on the next day he was to envisage alternative futures as right for him. In each case, he should give freedom to his imagination and pause wherever he found his feelings touched. He was to seek the positive reasons and emotions in each possibility. As each picture developed and filled itself in, he was also to pray for the light of God to shine through the glass, so to speak. Or, to change the metaphor, he was to hold the Geiger counter of himself and his responses over each alternative, allowing the implications of each choice to sink in. By being aware of his feelings and of the more objective pros and cons, he could watch the needle of the Geiger counter of the self. Then on the third day he was to come back to prayer and to weigh before God which of the two alternatives spoke more powerfully to him or left him with more lasting peace. Where was there a stronger sense of rightness?

Described in this way, the whole thing may seem strange and elaborate. Its strength and wisdom is that it avoids the confusions of "on the one hand...but on the other hand." This constant to-and-fro reminds me of people following the ball at a tennis match; in decision making it is counter-productive. But with this suggested method of discernment, there is time to listen with the heart, and in prayer, to listen to both sides before coming to weigh the two responses.

In Tony's case it turned out to be simple. Approaching the question in a prayerful spirit, he found that when he envisaged being married to someone other than Helen, it appealed only to his "adolescent self," as he called it. When he tried to imagine other possibilities, such as a religious vocation, he again found that it was attractive but not for him. On reflection, he began to suspect that his unease over the marriage commitment might have been provoked by an unresolved guilt over leaving the seminary several years before. When he came to the "window" of marriage with Helen, the sense of rightness was unmistakable, and further blessed with a deep gratitude before God. Clearly, in this case there was little need for the weighing of issues planned for the third day. But it was wiser to do it just the same, to protect the decision against later moments of insecurity.

As in other examples mentioned, Tony's discovery needed a deeper listening to his own experience than was possible under pressure. Like many a person faced with a major step in life, he was buffeted by a certain panic and by lingering self-doubts. His important insight was that within himself were two distinct levels of response, one mature and in tune, the other superficial and immature. It is the old contrast between the true and the false self in everyone. What is called discernment simply means learning to read the contrast, to sift the levels, to recognize the roots in the light of the fruits.

The Spirit at Work

When pondering the dangers of darkness earlier, I mentioned the practical wisdom of Ignatius Loyola—about not changing direction in the dark. I want to draw on him again to cast light on this whole business of making decisions as a believer. In his _Spiritual Exercises_, Ignatius assumes that the road to making good decisions will seldom be smooth and that it will require some careful preparing of the ground. If the heart is to be free, it will have to confront its unfreedoms. If I am to avoid the deceptions of the Herods inside and outside me, I will need some grace like the dream of the Magi. One of the simplest and most important assumptions of Ignatius is that God is at work within each person's experience, and that it requires only a careful listening and a certain liberation to become aware of the "movements" of the "good spirit." For many people this is revolutionary. If they have grown up with a religion that keeps God distant or with a view of revelation as utterly over and done with, they will never think of God as acting *now* in their lives. If so, they will never trust their own deep experience as a place where the Spirit continues to speak and guide. "Where is your God?" Yet another answer is possible: God is within you and can be recognized where God's Spirit and your spirit meet.

To say this is only to echo key moments in the New Testament. The night before he died, Jesus promised his friends that he would be present to them in three new ways: in the bread and wine; in the love of one another; and in the coming of the Paraclete. This third gift is the one that Jesus spoke of most at the supper, as if to stress that his absence would open the door to a new and deeper presence. Physically his friends will see him no longer. Spiritually this "other Paraclete" will continue to be "with" and "within" them "always" (John 14:16-17). Even the word "other" is revealing: it implies that Jesus himself was the first Paraclete and that his work will continue in a new way.

What then does this word "paraclete" mean? Its root meaning is "advocate," literally someone called alongside to plead on one's behalf, like a defense lawyer in a trial. The whole setting in John's gospel implies that the friends of Jesus are going on trial, that they will run into trouble in the "world," but that they will have this attorney and witness to defend them and to guide them "to all truth" (John 16:13). They will have a new consoler to encourage them and "remind" them of Jesus (John 14:26).

Biblical experts have written volumes on these short passages but the core message is clear. It is that Jesus promises to continue to live within humanity in a new and real way, dwelling in each person through his Spirit. This is the basis of the confidence of Ignatius Loyola that we can experience the movements of the Spirit, and that these will guide us toward good decisions. If the richness of this vision comes alive for a person, then religion changes its wavelength. It is no longer a matter only of church membership or of duties to a distant God or of keeping commandments. All of these have their place, but once the Spirit becomes real for a person, faith deepens into something at once personal and more than personal. In the depths of each self, to borrow an image from St. Paul, we are being shaped into "God's work of art," into the goodness that is meant to be "our way of life" (Ephesians 2:10). The Spirit is that sculptor working away on the granite of our humanity, and it is possible to recognize the Spirit by its fruits: love, joy, peace, patience, kindness, goodness, trustfulness, gentleness, and self-control (Galatians 5:19-22).

This is what Ignatius called the experience of consolation as opposed to the experience of desolation, and although he expects people to run into conflicts where these two moods tussle together, he assumes that consolation will win and that it is the normal experience for a Christian. It is also the touchstone for any decision. If an inner joy calls and draws one to goodness, and if it lasts, then, says Ignatius with disarming directness, we can trust that the good spirit guides us. It is a startling claim for those who have never learned, when they experience a vague sense that they have lost God, to trust their own experience as an answer to the question, Where is your God? But it is a liberating insight that translates the gospel promise of the Spirit into each person's experience.

All this is simpler than the many words we use to explain it. I recall, with a certain comic embarrassment, an incident when I was studying theology. We had a professor, a man of both learning and sanctity who hated eloquent frills of any kind. He taught a course on grace, and at the end of the year there was a fifteen minute oral examination on the topic. I had put a lot of work into the course and thought I was well prepared. The professor quizzed me up and down and, seeing that I knew the areas reasonably well, threw in a deceptively simple question, "What does grace do to a person?" I responded with the views of all sorts of authorities from St. Augustine to Karl Rahner, from Thomas Aquinas to Edward Schillebeeckx. To no avail. He interrupted me on every route with "But what does grace *do* to a person?" Eventually the clock ended my agony. "Time's up," he said with a certain satisfaction. "Grace *changes* a person. Goodbye now."

To return to the imagery of the Magi, the dream is what changes their plan. That is the moment of the Spirit's intervention to save them. Perhaps God intervenes only in ways like this, changing hearts through the Spirit, not working magic in an external way. For us, too, the dream protects us from Herod's lies and guides us toward the love story that we are asked to live. We find, to our surprise, that the dream of God coincides with our own deepest desires. It is only to the false self—the self that Herod hypnotizes—that God seems an enemy. But when we reach the cave of our hearts, God's hopes and our hopes mingle and merge. We can now propose in yet another way that we have not lost God. *God is where the two dreams meet, God's and ours.*

CHAPTER ELEVEN

ANOTHER WAY: JUSTICE

The last words of the Magi story, "they went home by another way," no doubt refer to their route back to the East and to the fact that they avoided returning to Herod. But in the poetry of the gospel, "way" seems to be a code word for the way of life that Christ called the Kingdom. It means a wholly different vision.

The Magi did not stay in Bethlehem; they went back to their own country. The end of their story is not known, even though many legends have been woven around them. What can be gleaned from the gospel text is that they returned home somehow changed in themselves; they had experienced a journey of awakening. They now had a different sense of God, something to shape the rest of their lives. But we are left guessing as to how they continued to find God, or how they remained faithful to what they had discovered.

How can I live the vision of God that I glimpse in Jesus? That is always a crucial question for faith but never more so than in our confused and crisis-ridden time. How can we find "another way" for today?

Martyrdom

In November 1989, I received a letter from an old friend; it came like a gift out of the blue. Conor describes himself as an unbeliever. Yet he wrote to sympathize with me over the deaths of my fellow Jesuits in El Salvador. "Taking the side of the poor and powerless is obviously as dangerous as it ever was. I find it profoundly moving and humbling that men like these are prepared to die for their commitment." Conor could have stopped there—with that generous tribute—but he did not. He went on to comment, "It's terribly easy to criticize the diversity of opinion and stance that makes up 'the church,' but there are still individuals within it who are genuinely Christ-like. They ask important questions of us all. I feel chastened and challenged."

So do I, needless to say. In that spirit I want to respond here to Conor's letter. Let me begin with what I call my _entonces_ insight. That word is one of the most ordinary of terms in Spanish, and means "then" or "and so," with some sense of cause. But this little word was at the center of an important insight that came to me on Friday, March 6, 1987.

I was in Maracaibo in Venezuela. It was the first week of Lent and the Scripture reading for Mass was Isaiah 58:1-9. It is one of those ironic passages where God, in the mouth of the prophet, is being sarcastic about how people observe the regulations of religion. "They seek me day after day," as if they wanted to know my hopes, and if they were living as I asked them to. Yet they complain that they receive no reward, that they have no sense of my being with them. What is the point of penance or fasting, if I seem to stay so distant? But take a hard look at this so-called fasting. It's an external exercise, a pretence of penance, of hanging the head and looking sad. But all the while workers are being oppressed, violence holds sway, and the poor are beaten up. (This is not an extract from an Amnesty International report but a close paraphrase of Isaiah.) The prophet goes on, speaking solemnly in the name of God: the real penance, and the one that I want from my people, is quite different. It would consist in liberating the oppressed, breaking the structures of injustice, lifting the burdens from the poor, sharing bread with the hungry, sheltering the homeless, clothing the naked, and not turning your back against your own people.

Live It First and Then...

What an extraordinary passage! But I have yet to come to my point. On that Friday in sweltering Maracaibo, I heard that call to genuine "fasting," as I had heard it many times before. Perhaps it had more drama for me because I was in Latin America. But I was not prepared for the impact of the next little word—*entonces*—and what it led to. In Spanish, the passage in Isaiah continues: *entonces brillará tu luz como el amanecer...entonces, si me llamas, yo te respondere "aqui estoy."* "Then let your light shine like the dawn...*then*, if you call me, I will answer, 'Here I am.'" And the rest of the chapter develops that powerful promise. It is full of the word "if." *If* you struggle against oppression, *then* you will find God. *If* you create a world of caring, *then* all the old gloom and darkness will lift, and you will experience the closeness of God.

What came home to me was a surprisingly different angle on the quest for faith. Something utterly obvious seemed to fall into place as I listened to that familiar reading: not only is love more important than faith, but love is *the* gateway to faith. Confronted by Isaiah's words, I discovered that I was putting the cart before the horse. I imagined faith to be mainly a question of truth, a question for the mind. To think things out may be vital, but it is not the key to faith. According to Isaiah, commitment to people comes first, and today that means taking one's place in the struggle to heal our world. Previously I was inclined to interpret people's faith problems as questions seeking answers, and to suppose that *after* a person found faith *then* he or she could begin to live it. But that "then" of mine is not the "then" of Isaiah. For him faith is more a form of love-truth than of reason-truth. The summary of his message would be: *live it and you will know.* Live the option to serve the weak and the wounded, and you will have fewer problems finding God. As Newman was to put it centuries later, "We believe because we love."

In many ways my _entonces_ insight is ridiculously simple and far from new, but it had taken me half a lifetime to grasp that the logic of faith is the reverse of what we are used to: we normally know things by working them out and verifying them. But faith is more an existential truth than an objective one. It is verified in practice rather than in theory. How I live in this world has a shaping influence on how I see the meaning of everything. If I live uncaringly or with self as an idol, then it is no surprise if God seems distant or irrelevant. We meet God most, whether we recognize it or not, through our lived options more than through the gestures of our religiousness. The practices of religion, in Isaiah's view, are authentic only when backed up with the hard currency of action. Such a stance and its cost in El Salvador moved Conor and gave him a sense of what was "Christ-like."

The Prophetic Note

The aim of many Old Testament prophets was to disturb the _status quo_ of the kings and priests, who settled too easily for a religion of external observance. The prophets' goal was to rescue religion from its rigidities and to fire again the imagination of believers. Typically they would awaken people to God's hopes by reminding them of the sufferings of the poor. Perhaps I heard this emphasis in my youth, and certainly I must have read these biblical passages. But it has only been in recent years, and through the stimulus of being in Latin America, that these challenges have caught fire for me. As Marx liked to say, context conditions consciousness. My context, the individualistic West, tended to restrict faith to a largely private sphere. Until I saw the world of the poor with my own eyes—as opposed to the frequent images of Third World pain on television—I was able to avoid the vehemence of that prophetic note.

But once discovered, this note sounded everywhere through the Scriptures. To take just one example from the New Testament:

I had read the letter of James many times but it was not until I read it prayerfully in San Felix, living across from Pedro Pablo's family, that James's bluntness struck me with new force. Take the irony of his remark that even the demons believe in God (James 2:19). By comparing them to devils, James is satirizing believers who think that faith is an abstract truth, unconnected with how they live.

On the contrary, he argues, without compassion faith is a dead thing. His whole second chapter is a disturbing text for the complacent believer, which could well mean most of us. Beware of treating people differently because of their social status. The poor have been chosen by God and are rich in faith. What use are kindly words toward those who are victimized? Unless you try to change their situation, your so-called faith is a hollow pretense. Don't just believe! Do something! Action is the only litmus paper for faith that James trusts, and the Conors of today seem to apply exactly the same test. They may remain shy of church and suspicious of mere words, but they glimpse the truth of faith when it is lived in options of solidarity.

SUMMARY

If the core of being a Christian means an alternative way of life, it also means a long battle with Herod—the Herod of ego within and of institutions and systems all around. Sometimes this option to live according to Kingdom values costs people their lives. Then, as Conor said, it becomes the strongest argument for faith. There is a relevant saying in John's gospel (3:21) that "whoever does the truth comes out into the light." We might adapt it for our contemporary situation of faith and doubt: what will most help those unsure, like Conor, to glimpse the light is the witness of believers who do the truth. For faith is less a theory than a commitment to share in the project that Jesus called the Kingdom, and that means a long transformation of hearts and of history.

Much energy and ink have been expended in defending God against atheism, and doing so on the level of theory. It is undoubtedly a useful debate, but sometimes little more than a debate. The more central question, in my experience, is not about the existence of God but about how faith can be lived in today's world. Credibility comes when livability is found, not the other way around. This book has been about people at various stages of that search for ways to live, and about how God, who seems absent too often, is really encountered in their struggles and experiences.

So, then, where is our God? What answers have we found? Several different and yet converging ones, all of them linked to moments in the Magi journey.

God is found through following the *light* that leads us into mystery. To find courage for that journey we often need some liberating awakening first to the wonder of existence and of our own selves.

God is found even through the *darkness* that is unavoidable along the way. This need not damage us if we trust that darkness is never the whole story and that we are never abandoned or alone in those shadows.

God is found by *questioning*, by honestly seeking to make sense of our experience. Some people get stuck with inadequate levels of questions and answers. Yet, approached with reverence, there are avenues of inquiry worthy both of us and of God.

God is found whole *walking side by side* along the road. We are not meant to travel alone. Faith blossoms through many kinds of community, and these are excitingly visible all around us today.

God is found in spite of *deceptions*, evils, and dangers in our path. Although Herod's twisted system rules the world, to recognize his trickery is half the battle. Then we become free for another kingship.

God is found in the *house* that is the church. For all its faults and failings, it offers a spiritual home, long tested by history. It is the place where the Spirit continues to guide the friends of Jesus, and where vast numbers of people find food for their journey.

God is found through *adoration* or prayer. We need simply to risk the strangeness of God's silence, where levels of deeper listening await us, and where the heart can learn a new logic of love.

God is found through *giving*. We are here for others, especially for the many wounded of our world. Anyone who tries to care in any way is not far from the kingdom, and in the evening of life, says John of the Cross, we will be judged by love.

God is found through *dreaming*, whenever revelation touches the depths of a person. This conversion of vision can happen in many ways—through Scripture, through sacraments, or through the slow artistry of the Spirit, shaping hearts and changing lives.

God is found by choosing *another way* of living in this world. It means embracing reality and entering into the struggles of history, great and small. For the Kingdom is here as well as hereafter, and a Christian is someone who dances to that different tune, first powerfully heard in the heart of Christ and now echoed unsteadily in each life and in the larger drama of healing this world.

Where is your God? There is an Eastern parable that portrays God as playing hide and seek with humanity. According to one version, God asks the angels for advice about the best place to hide. Go to the farthest star. Try the depths of the sea. What about some inaccessible cave or desert? One angel more subtly suggests that God might find the best disguise among the poor. But eventually one wise old angel (or are angels ageless?) comes up with another idea. "Hide at the center of human experience, where the heart meets reality. Hide yourself at the cutting edge where people shape their lives." According to the parable, this is the solution chosen by God.

I hope this book has been in tune with that tale. It, too, has tried to glimpse God in those places where people change and grow, where they let themselves be reached by the cry of others, where they listen and learn compassion, where they struggle and pay the price of love. We have not lost God. God is in the shaping moments of our human experience, at the turning points of our story, as the axis of our adventure in this world.

EPILOGUE

Several of the themes of this book are beautifully captured in a totally different medium, in Ermanno Olmi's *Cammina Cammina*. As I mentioned earlier, this is a unique presentation of the Magi story in a full length feature film and one that brings a marvelous freshness to that familiar tale. Not only does it show the quest of the traditional three wise men. They are accompanied by their tribes on a chaotic pilgrimage that mingles reverence and irreverence. The heart of the film is both deeply spiritual (like Olmi's masterpiece *The Tree of the Wooden Clogs*) and gently satiric about what formal religion does to revelation.

At the outset, the young son of Mel, the rabbi-astronomer, protests loudly against sacrificing a lamb as an offering to God, and throughout the film there are recurring moments of debate as to what kind of God they are searching for. At one point a strange, prophetic figure in the mountains mocks the pilgrims for seeking a god who would be their slave, whereas he is "waiting for a God of joy, a friend." The moment of finding Jesus with Mary and Joseph is handled with great tenderness, but immediately after Mel comments that people will wonder why God comes "in such poverty," he holds a service of thanksgiving during which a collection is taken up among the crowd.

A little later, and with one of the shifts of mood typical of Olmi, one of the most significant conversations of the entire piece takes place between the interpreter (for the Magi speak different languages) and Mel. "Do you believe in God?" asks the linguist, adding, "Most people who believe in God have their eyes turned to the sky, but you're always looking at the earth." Mel quotes a saying in response, "Lift a stone and thou shalt find me. Chop wood and I will be there." It is reminiscent of that comic moment at the opening of the Acts of the Apostles when the disciples after the Ascension are portrayed "staring into the sky" and are rebuked by two divine messengers (Acts 1:10). The implication is that God will be found in reality, not in some purely spiritual realm.

But in what reality will God be found? That is the final source of conflict in *Cammina Cammina*: The three Magi have the same disturbing dream, and realize that "the mighty in this world" will go to any lengths "to stop people finding their King." So they decide to leave for home, even if it means traveling through the night. But the interpreter bursts into angry protest against their self-concern, and offers another version of the significance of their dream. "It's now that God is asking us for help." In his view, they should go back to defend the child even at the risk of their own lives. "God has no need of our help," says Mel in shocked response; his great plan is to build a temple to commemorate their discovery of the infant King.

This scene enacts a perennial clash between two spiritualities, one of unworldly transcendence, the other of involvement in the struggles of history. The interpreter continues to insist that we serve God with more than "words and signs," so he rides back alone to try to save the child. He travels through scenes of carnage, with dead mothers and children strewn everywhere, until finally he comes to the stable where they had all seen Jesus with Mary and Joseph. There is nobody there now, only a lamb bleating; but unlike the surrounding area, there are no signs of blood in the stable. The camera then switches to the Magi arriving home in triumph, and thus the film ends with ambiguity.

Is it enough to recognize God in Jesus, and then to celebrate that reality? Or are we to risk the danger zone in order to protect the child from Herod? Where is our God? Yet another variation suggests itself: Far from being lost to us, God is where the visions of the heart and the struggles of reality meet and where that meeting gives life and bears fruit.